TURN THAT DOWN!

A Hysterical History of Rock, Roll, Pop, Soul, Punk, Funk, Rap, Grunge, Motown, Metal, Disco, Techno, *and* other Forms *of* Musical Aggression through the Ages

LEWIS GROSSBERGER

TURN THAT DOWN!

A Hysterical History of Rock, Roll, Pop, Soul, Punk, Funk, Rap, Grunge, Motown, Metal, Disco, Techno, *and* other Forms *of* Musical Aggression through the Ages

LEWIS GROSSBERGER

emmis humor

This man is the very embodiment of the spirit of rock and roll. And yet, he has dropped his microphone again and cannot seem to find it.

 To Joyce

An insubordinate subdivision of Emmis Books

The Old Firehouse 1700 Madison Road Cincinnati, OH 45206
www.emmisbooks.com/humor

Library of Congress Control Number 2005923530

Manufactured in the United States of America
Cover, book, and stamp designs by Gregory Hischak

First Edition
10 9 8 7 6 5 4 3 2 1

TURN THAT DOWN!

A Hysterical History of Rock, Roll, Pop, Soul, Punk, Funk, Rap, Grunge, Motown, Metal, Disco, Techno, and Other Forms of Musical Aggression Through the Ages

Table of Contents

X

Preface
to the
Foreword

This is a book about the dominant music of the last half of the twentieth century. For lack of a better phrase, I call it rock and roll, though it has many names, including rhythm and blues, heavy metal, soul, rap, punk, funk, grunge, pop, hip, hop, Heinrich von Papen (only in parts of eastern Bavaria), and, of course, a phrase more often screamed than whispered, *Turn That Down!*

Where did this music come from? Where did it go? What is its meaning in the grand scheme of things? These are just a few of the questions I have evaded in the course of this work. Instead, I have concentrated on all the sex, drugs, violence, and scandalous rumors in the world of rock and roll, or whatever it's called, since every indicator tells us that's what really interests readers and makes them put their credit cards on the counter.

As a historian (and I trust history will someday confirm that I am one despite the angry outcry from my many critics) I have relied not on original sources, who are notoriously unreliable since most of them are dead, or on secondary sources, who are twice as unreliable, but rather on unnamed sources. These are people who can say what needs to be said without fear of quibblers pestering them with annoying questions.

Also, I have made up a lot of stuff because, let's face it, that is much more fun than wading through old books and articles or interviewing self-promoting bores. I do believe in truth—passionately so—but only in small amounts. As any successful writer can tell you, too much truth will invariably ruin a good story.

Observant readers may detect some minor biases on the part of the author—for instance, my belief that there were hardly any good rock songs written after 1974 nor any pop tunes worth mentioning written after 1960. But the only practical effect of such an approach was to make the book much shorter than it would otherwise have been and surely that is not entirely a bad thing.

A brief word about wording: There are those who insist against all logic that the phrase "rock and roll" should be written "rock 'n' roll," not "rock and roll." These people have some kind of apostrophe fetish and I will never give in to such special interests. As for the corrupt ampersand crowd, with their constant lobbying in favor of "rock & roll," I can only say, "#@*&$ them."

Finally—and by that of course I mean penultimately—I would like to thank all those who tried to help me in the completion of this book. How I wish they had succeeded.

So now, as the light dims and ghostly images swim before me, these terrible specters from my past trying to drive me mad with horror and regret, I say, On with the fun!

Lewis Grossberger, Tupelo, New York

Introduction
to the
Prologue

"Rock and roll," goes the old song, **"is here to stay and** that's why I love rock-and-roll music, any old way you choose it." Ain't it the truth.

Rock and roll and its many derivatives, such as coal tar, has been (or is it have been? You tell me) the most dynamic, exciting, and unpredictable force in popular culture for the past half century, not counting television, movies, sex, and professional wrestling.

Like all important art, popular or un-, rock and roll speaks directly to the heart, as well as its valves, and gives voice to those powerful universal impulses that we all do our best to conceal, for fear of arrest followed by a harsh prison term.

But it would be a mistake to think that rock and roll is only music. For it is also lyrics. Of course the lyrics are often incomprehensible, but never doubt that they are there, even in the case of instrumentals, in which the lyrics are *thought*, rather than sung.

The words may be smart or dumb; they may be slurred, drawled, drooled, or perfectly enunciated (unlikely, I admit); but they are always telling us, with all the frantic urgency that only rock and roll can impart, that human beings are still in the world and still making a mess of it. This is a message we need to hear since to forget it would be to risk thinking we aren't a bunch of hopeless idiots, which of course we are. No other art form, foreign or domestic, has ever captured this profound truth as well as rock and roll (with the possible exception of finger painting).

It is now more than half a century since rock and roll came rocking and rolling into rambunctious existence, which means, among other things, that we are terribly old. Most of us, anyway. Me. You, I don't care that much about.

Many of us forget, and many more of us have never known, what the world was like before rock and roll. It was a lot quieter, of course, and a lot duller, too, except when a world war was in progress. Most of the time, things were in black and white, car radiators boiled over frequently, and, incredibly, *every single telephone in the nation was connected to the wall by a cord.* This was the sordid, repressive climate that the pioneers of rock and roll had to overcome and the fact that they did, and without even noticing they were doing it, is almost beyond belief.

Nor is rock (as it is sometimes called by those who forget that rock and roll rolls as well as rocks) purely a local phenomenon anymore. In today's world of instant communications, of iPods, e-mail, and free condom distribution to the promiscuous, whenever a riot, street fight, or genocide commences, it's a safe bet that it's being played out to a rock beat. Without rock, even the Muzak we now bop to in elevators and malls would be stuck forever in some aspic of bland sonic mucus that time forgot and the black leather jacket would be confined to museums of ancient apparel instead of being proudly flaunted on every street corner.

Yet to describe the history of rock, with or without roll, has its pitfalls, and no one who has ever fallen into a pit is eager to repeat the experience, especially if it was lined with punji stakes. That is because rock, unlike, say, a chocolate cupcake with a vanilla cream center, lacks an *identifiable consistency of form.* The damn thing simply won't stay the same for more than a minute. Every new generation has carried rock and roll to a place the previous generation would have found uninhabitable, especially in November with all that cold rain. The screaming, pants-wetting Elvis fan of 1954, if subjected to Boy George's Culture Club of 1983 or Phish in 2002, would collapse, bleeding profusely from the ears and nose and moaning, "Please, someone dial 911."

Despite its elusive character as a swirling, formless morass of patternless ephemera without any claim to formal artistic unity (much like the food in high-school cafeterias), rock and roll has persevered because of one powerful, redeeming quality: the ability to unite a group of glum, bored, surly young people into a rowdy, sweaty mass of dancing, frenzied, sex-crazed hooligans.

It is this and this alone that has ensured rock's survival in an era when most people would rather sit at home and watch television than track the swift gazelle across the savannah with bow and poison-tipped arrow. Today, with the shadow of terrorism fallen menacingly across the horizon, one can only wonder whether rock and roll still brandishes enough *mojo* (one of the many strange expressions we shall encounter on our musical journey) to keep our youth from crawling into deep holes in the ground and curling up permanently in the fetal position. It is a great deal to ask of any pop art form, to be sure.

Indeed, probably too much.

And ain't that a shame?

Lewis Grossberger, still in Tupelo, New York

LEWIS GROSSBERGER

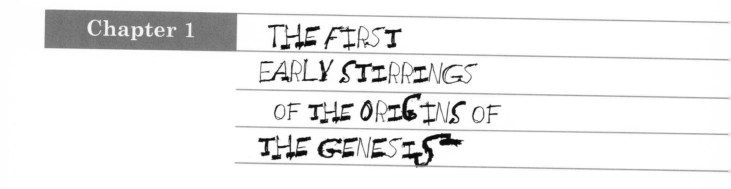

Chapter 1

THE FIRST EARLY STIRRINGS OF THE ORIGINS OF THE GENESIS

Rock and roll was invented by black people living in the southeastern part of the United States, though at the time it wasn't called rock and roll and they weren't called black people. (Nor were the states all that united, if you really want to know the truth.)

Hard as it may be to believe today, the black people were then called Negroes (except by Southern white people, who pronounced it somewhat differently) and they were oppressed—so oppressed that they had to make music constantly to keep from being depressed. Neither did it help much that they were living in places like Hog Snot, Alabama.

Unfortunately, there was little music available in this culturally backward region. In fact, outside of gospel, jazz, ragtime, swing, spirituals, country, western, country-western, bluegrass, Dixieland, blues, rhythm, rhythm and blues, bebop, zydeco, hillbilly, Cajun, folk, calypso, reggae, chamber music, semi-classical, Broadway show tunes, jug-band music, hillbilly-funk, and baroque string-quartet recitals, there wasn't a single thing worth humming.

Thus it was necessary for these downtrodden folk to create an entirely new means of musical expression, one that would enable them to express their more subtle emotional states such as horniness.

To do this, they naturally turned to the most oppressed segment of the oppressed community, the Blind Guitar Pickers. Only they were beaten down enough to give the downbeat.

Amp Up Your Rockabulary

Riff: A musical passage that is longer than a note but briefer than a rock opera.

Gig: Half a giggle.

Man: *(obsolete)* A word mandatorily placed at the end or beginning of every sentence uttered during the '60s and '70s. Later replaced by "dude," "yo," and "so, like, whatever."

Mojo: A very useful—indeed almost magical—word that can be used whenever one has little or nothing to say. Some examples: "Got any mojo, dude? I'm all out." "Those old guys, they had mojo! Not like these wannabes now." "Anybody know how to get to Mojo from here?"

Hook: A memorable bit that captures a listener's attention, turning an otherwise mediocre song into a hit. For example: a clever lyric, an unusual instrument or sound effect, six men yelling "tequila," a kennel of barking dogs, or someone singing on key.

Cover: To steal.

Soul: A quality I got and you ain't.

It is not known exactly which Blind Guitar Picker picked out the first rock rock-and-roll song or even whether he was really blind (Some of them were faking it to attract blind-guitar-picker groupies) but what is known is that whoever it was definitely had a colorful nickname. Most music historians believe that it was either Big Bad Bill "Boozy Boy" Bagley or Sandy Rivers who plunked that fateful first note, though other music historians insist it was Howlin' Wolf, Bo Diddley, Muddy Waters, Fats Domino, Catfish Hunter, or Judge Learned Hand.

Of the first group, a minority faction contends that Bagley played the first rock song, Rivers played the first roll song and on one climactic day, they got together for a duet.

In any event, both performers had started out as blues shouters, a singing style popular in roadhouses catering to the hard of hearing. They hailed from the Mississippi Delta but got tired of the hailstorms and moved to Chicago in the 1940s when assured there were no cotton fields there. After word got out that one or both of them, or possibly someone else entirely, was rocking to a hot new beat,[1] other Southern musicians decided that they wanted to quit jamming to cool old licks and join in. In fact, so many moved that a new railroad, the Mississippi and Chicago, had to be built to carry them, their relatives, and their managers.

---

1. There is one anthropologist who swears that rock and roll was actually invented by George Washington Carver in 1897, but that Carver saw no use for it and put it away in a drawer. There it languished for more than half a century, occasionally giving out a poignant little thump.

Due to this extraordinary new urban migration and the post-war economic boom, Chicago and other Midwestern cities such as Oshkosh and Kalamazoo soon employed thousand of workers in huge jazz factories or rhythm-and-blues assembly plants. Some of the more talented music workers were actually able to take a blue note and push it through a horn till it was worn into a new note.

At the time most of these unheralded and semiheralded artists thought they were playing rhythm and blues, but it turned out they were wrong. Musicologists today agree that the difference between rock and roll and rhythm and blues is vast although no one has ever been able to figure out exactly what it is.

Once informed that they had invented an important new art form, these musicians, highly intuitive but without formal education, sensed that they only had about a week to write and perform as many classic rock-and-roll songs as they could before a horde of white guys with smart accountants came along and ripped them off. Not wishing to miss this golden opportunity, they took enormous quantities of drugs to help them work faster. Thus began one of rock and roll's most venerable and hallowed traditions, one that endures to this very day.

Only known photograph of legendary Mississippi Delta blues singer Yelpin' Catfish, circa 1937. Behind him is Elsworth Tubbs, Catfish's spokesman. Pathologically shy, Catfish spoke only to Tubbs, who spoke to no one.

Chapter 2

A Wop Bop A... Whatever

Two of the most influential performers in the Early Days of Rock and Roll were Little Richard and Chuck Berry. It is even possible that they invented rock and roll, despite what you read in the previous chapter.

There are some historians who believe they are one and the same person, though that is regarded by most as a dangerously radical viewpoint. A quick way of telling them apart in an emergency is that Chuck Berry is the one who walks like a duck, while Little Richard is apt to suddenly exclaim, often in midsentence, "A wop bop a lubop a lop bam boom" or possibly "A wop bop a loo mop a wop bam boom." Interpretations differ on the exact pronunciation, as well as the definition. (I stand with those who believe the phrase derives from an ancient French expression meaning, "Perhaps I am growing a bit overexcited now, am I not?")

Both men achieved the distinction of living longer than anyone else in the history of rock and roll and may still be alive even now, though that would, of course, be impossible to prove.

Little Richard was born in Tupelo, Mississippi, the son of Big Richard and his wife, Medium. He was named Little because as a baby he was very small, about the size of an infant, in fact. His sister, Long Tall Sally, grew faster than he did, and was later immortalized in song by her shorter brother, who was impressed with her height as well as her length, believing them to be two different things.

Wearing mascara, sporting the highest pompadour ever seen on a human being before the birth of Lyle Lovett, and screaming in a piercing falsetto that made household pets psychotic for miles around, Little Richard was occasionally mistaken for an alien species and brought to the White House to meet the President, who would pledge interplanetary peace and present him with a gold tie clip. For his part, Little would usually reply, "Tutti frutti, all rootie," which Pentagon language experts puzzled over for months.

Growing exhausted from these constant trips to the nation's capital, Little retired at the height of his career (about five foot eleven) after God appeared to him in a vision and suggested, "Shut up!" He became a minister in the Sixth Day Adventist church because its services were shorter than those of the Seventh Day Adventist Church. Preaching there, he warned parishioners that rock and roll was sinful because it could lead to singing and dancing. But he found his addiction hard to kick and made a comeback every year for the rest of his life. "I am confused," he told interviewers, "but sincere."

Even at this very early stage in the life of rock and roll, Little signaled that rock performers would challenge society's rigid prevailing view of sexual identity. At the time only two genders were permitted to exist: male and female. Today, of course, there are dozens, with more being discovered daily and distinctive makeup available to all. This is Little Richard's legacy and he can be proud.

To avoid being recognized, Little Richard would dress more sedately in public than he did onstage, as shown here in a London airport in 1969.

Short-Shrift Profiles

Bo Diddley

Contrary to popular belief, Bo Diddley is not related to P. Diddy or Bo Derek. The facts are these: He grew up in Chicago. He used a square-bodied guitar. He is almost as legendary as Chuck Berry and Little Richard but not quite. His sound is more raw, darker and diddlier. He invented the Bo Diddley beat, a rockin', boppin', insect-stompin' sound which is rumored to mean something obscene in Morse code. It has been copied many times by many musicians and several armies. Bo is the only famous rocker to have recorded a hit song whose title is his name. That song is called "Bo Diddley." He has not died yet even though he is quite old.

In fact, there is now speculation among rock anthropologists that Little Richard was an early, experimental form of Michael Jackson.

Chuck Berry's real name was Buck Cherry, but due to a bout of childhood dyslexia, he always introduced himself as Chuck Berry and the name stuck, despite frantic efforts to remove it with alcohol, turpentine, and ammonia-based cleaners.

While fooling around with a borrowed pencil one day, Chuck invented the trick of writing and singing one's own songs. This later became a necessity for any rocker worth his salt, though at the time salt wasn't worth very much. The advantage of such double creativity was that it allowed the recording industry to rip off a black artist *twice*.

Though never himself a teenager, having been born at the age of 39 (in Tupelo, Mississippi), Chuck wrote many songs that teenagers loved, such as "Sweet Little Sixteen" and "Roll Over, Beethoven," which dealt with the great classical composer's wife, Maybelline, and her struggle to make her deaf husband give her more space in their tiny bed.

Sometimes in trouble with the law, Chuck Berry spent time in jails and reform schools, usually on trumped-up charges, such as "transporting an underage guitar into a white neighborhood for immoral purposes." His famous duckwalk was in fact designed to fool the guards into believing he was a harmless farm animal out for a stroll, thus allowing an escape. It did not work, but it helped make Chuck Berry the legend that he is today, inspiring such younger talents as Keith Richards, Regis Philbin, and an entire generation of psychohistorians who have been trying ever since to figure out exactly why he continues trying to walk like a duck.

Though he easily could have become an embittered and resentful man after his victimization by the white power structure, instead, because of his largeness of spirit, Chuck Berry ended up just a bit on the grouchy side. Of course, once officially recognized as a God of Rock and Roll in 1989, he insisted on being paid upfront in gold bullion for all engagements and having his boots licked by record executives daily—but really, who among us would behave any differently?

In his later years, Chuck Berry would sometimes get stuck in this position. Once he had to duckwalk six miles through heavy traffic to a chiropractor's house.

Chapter 3

LOOK OUT!
HERE COME
THOSE CRAZY
WHITE PEOPLE

In 1953, President Harry S. Truman seized the nation's steel mills to foil a threatened strike and subsequently the Supreme Court declared his action unconstitutional. This has nothing to do with rock and roll but it is an interesting historical fact to mull over when you get some free time.

More relevant to our story were the hordes of restless teenagers roaming America's schools and malt shops[1] in the 1950s. The teenager had been invented only as recently as the previous decade by the automobile industry, which needed somebody to buy jalopies[2] that no sane adult would touch. Before that, teenagers were just children and no one paid them the slightest attention. But now, something had gone wrong somewhere and suddenly there were millions of them and they dressed funny. Their parents were desperately frightened, though they did not dare show it because once a teenager senses fear, you are finished.

Now that the nation had millions of sexually aroused teenagers driving around in loud cars with radios and bad mufflers, they could not be kept pacified with Patti Page singing "How Much Is That Doggie in the Window?" This sort of song was the pop music of the era and to hear just a couple of bars is to understand that some sort of violent revolution was inevitable.

1. A type of shop where malt was sold. No longer in existence.
2. Dysfunctional used cars. Still in existence.

In fact, had rock and roll not come along at this precise moment in history, the teenage population would have turned Communist and brought down the government out of sheer boredom by 1956. Thus we can safely say that rock and roll saved freedom and democracy. We're not actually going to say it but we could if we wanted to.

So far, the rock and roll being created by the various black performers segregated to Chapters 1 and 2 was not allowed admittance to the car radios of the millions of white teenagers driving around in this chapter. But rumors of its existence had begun to leak out, especially when people in the black community turned up their Victrolas.[3]

These two explosive elements, the car radio and the rock and roll, were finally introduced to each other by a man named Alan Freed. They immediately fell in love, dated, and had sex (of the unsafe variety).

Alan Freed was a disc jockey, first in Cleveland and then in New York. He had discovered rock and roll one fateful day when he took a wrong turn off a highway and accidentally drove into a black-only culvert where B.B. King (another giant of early rock and roll who I should have mentioned in Chapter 1 but forgot) was entertaining three hobos, a tramp, and a drifter. "Cool," said Freed, as it was March and a stiff wind was blowing through the culvert.

Fascinated by this new sound (the music, not the wind), Freed went to a black record store and bought up stacks and stacks of hot wax. When he played them the next day on his radio program, "The Alan Freed Slow Waltz Hour," the station manager rushed into his studio and screamed, "What the hell is that crap? It's too loud! It's nothing but noise! It's degenerate filth that will bring down this country! Plus I can't understand the words!" (Interestingly, that was the exact reaction of every white parent who heard the new music from then on.)

---

3. A type of machine that played something called a "record." No longer in existence. Either one.

Freed merely shrugged and pointed out the window. On the street stood 150,000 teenagers, holding transistor radios[4] to their ears, screaming deliriously, dancing, holding up lit candles, wetting themselves, and salaaming in the direction of Freed. The station manager took one look and said, "Oh, okay. No problem."

From that moment on, nothing would ever be the same.

Okay, maybe a few things.

Legendary DJ Alan Freed was the first producer to pay people to attend his live rock-and-roll shows. The unorthodox tactic worked brilliantly, except in a financial sense.

4. A new invention, developed by the Army in 1949 as a way of giving soldiers orders when they were apart from their commanders, but converted to civilian use when it turned out the soldiers were presenting them to girls in exchange for sex. No longer in existence.

All Your Problems Solved by Rock and Roll

Is this your predicament?	Then this is your solution.
You're a broken-hearted lover whose baby left you.	*Cry away your gloom at Heartbreak Hotel. (It's down at the end of Lonely Street.)*
You're sittin' here singin' the blues.	*Let me take you on a sea cruise.*
A song that brings back memories of your baby is filling your heart with pain.	*Don't play it no more.*
You need someone to care.	*Just call, I'll be there.*
They treat your baby mean and cruel, they try to keep you apart.	*You've gotta find a place to hide with your baby by your side.*
You hate blue Monday, got to work like a slave all day.	*Hang on till Saturday morning, oh, Saturday morning!*
You got a girl who lives on the hill; she won't love you.	*Her sister will.*
You've been a flop with chicks since 1956.	*You need love potion number nine.*
You feel blue in the night and you need her to hold you tight	*Whenever you want her, all you have to do is dream.*
She was gonna be your wife and you were gonna be her man but she let another guy come between you and it ruined your plans.	*Shout "Help, help me, Rhonda" and maybe Rhonda will come to help you get her out of your mind.*
You feel that you can't go on because all your hope is gone and your life is filled with confusion and happiness is just an illusion and your world is tumblin' down.	*Reach out, reach out for me.*

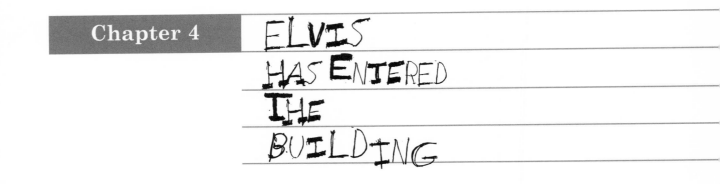

Chapter 4

ELVIS HAS ENTERED THE BUILDING

Elvis Amadeus Presley was born in Tupelo, Mississippi, in 1935, the son of a truck driver, Vernon Presley, and a sewing-machine oiler, Gladys Presley, who were, by an odd coincidence, married to each other. Interestingly, he had a twin brother who was stillborn. Because the brother was named Enos, Elvis objected throughout his life to the nickname "Elvis the Pelvis."

In 1948, the Presleys moved to Memphis, Tennessee, in search of better sex, and despite the parents' best efforts, Elvis followed them. Though the family was poor, it had little money—so little that it couldn't even afford a home on the wrong side of the tracks, instead living between them.

As a young boy, Elvis skipped school on Sundays, not realizing it was closed, and sneaked into black churches to listen to gospel, which he instinctively understood was a type of music. Elvis was gifted that way. Though he was tragically Caucasian, the congregation accepted his presence, fondly referring to him as "that dumb white kid" and sometimes allowing him to sweep up after the service if he paid them a few dollars. At night, he would listen to radio station WNVL in Nashville, often singing along with Jack Benny or the Lone Ranger.

By the time he was a teenager, Elvis was already tapping his foot so vigorously he had aroused the suspicions of the local police, who kept him under surveillance 24 hours a day, forwarding reports to FBI director J. Edgar Hoover on the boy's potentially subversive raw sexuality. Undeterred, Elvis bought a battered secondhand guitar and taught himself to play it, even though it lacked strings. On weekends, he hung out on Beale Street, an area frequented by black rhythm-and-blues artists, who used his head as a bongo drum. With his greasy "ducktail" haircut (so named because it resembled the tail of a duck), his black leather jacket, and his switchblade knife, Elvis was very popular among his teachers and fellow students at John Dillinger High School. In fact, they voted him Most Likely to Bring Rock and Roll to White America and Then Die in His Garishly Decorated Bathroom, Probably from Gluttony and Drug Abuse, a Bloated Parody of His Former Self.

After graduation, Elvis worked as a mechanical-bull repairman, a singing gondolier, a hamburger helper, a long-order cook, a bottle opener, a pipe cleaner, an art-museum docent, and at

The young Elvis sadly bids his mom and dad goodbye, explaining that he must leave home and enter show business so that he can get more girls.

other typical low-paying, dead-end jobs before making a decision that would Change the Course of History: he would cut a record as a birthday present for his beloved mom (who was still Gladys Presley). To do this, he went to a Memphis recording studio owned by a Memphis recording-studio owner named Sam Phillips. For years, Phillips had told people, "If I can find me a white man who can sing like a black man, stay out of jail for a few years, and isn't too ugly or over 65 years of age or married to his 12-year-old sister, and maybe shakes his hips some, I can be a millionaire and probably make a lot of money as well."

Elvis went into a recording booth and sang what some rock historians regard as the First Rock and Roll Song Ever Recorded by a White Person, while others regard it as the third and still others dismiss it as "pop schlock, though with an overlay of kitsch and a soupçon of schmaltz." At any rate, it went like this:

> *Happy birthday to you*
> *Happy birthday to you*
> *Happy birthday, my beloved, saintly, and adored mama,*
> *Happy birthday to you*[1]

---

1. The song, with its worship of the maternal parent, common to boys from Italy and the American South, was written in 1944 by Big Papa Lambeen, a cakewalking blues screamer who performed under the name Edwin Arnold J Johnson Jr., and who influenced Little Richard and Perry Como. Elvis had most likely heard it sung by a prison chain gang that liked to hang out near his home, harmonizing while they busted rocks and ate grits, or possibly the other way around.

Flabbergasted by what he had heard—an effortless fusion of R&B, C&W, M&Ms, pop, soda, and Jelly Roll Morton—Phillips rushed into the studio with a five-man band and three backup singers, tied Elvis to the microphone and demanded that he record a full album before releasing the dazed young man. Always polite to his elders, despite his menacing "hood" appearance, Elvis replied, according to one eyewitness, "Yes, sir, I sure will mumble mumble mumble if that's what you mumble," and poured out his young heart in song as he never had before and probably didn't even then.

The title of the album produced by Phillips's Sun Records, *Elvis Explodes Out of Nowhere and Takes the World by Storm,* was prophetic. Each of the dozen now-famous songs on it, including "That's All Right, Mama," "Never You Mind What Mama and I Are Doin', Papa," "Hound Dog," "Heartbreak Hotel," "Don't Be Cruel," and "If I Were a Rich Man,"[2] became number one hits simultaneously, the first time that this had ever happened in the history of the world.[3]

2. On which Elvis substituted the phrase "Oh, baby, yeah, baby, yeah, baby, yeah!" for the "didle didle didle didle dums" familiar to fans of the Broadway musical *Fiddler on the Roof*, from which it came.

3. Though in 1993, the same songs, recorded by The Three Tenors, on their album *The Three Tenors Shamelessly Rip Off Elvis and Sound Ridiculous While Doing It*, sold twice as many copies as Elvis's version did.

Chapter 5

THE BUILDING BURNS DOWN

CAUTION

This chapter contains graphic descriptions of Elvis's weird mating habits. *For mature readers only.*

Sam Phillips had big plans for Elvis but unfortunately lost him in a poker game to Colonel Tom Parker,[1] a highly decorated Salvation Army combat veteran and the most important trainer of performing seals in Arkansas. After tossing Elvis a few herrings, Parker promptly flew to New York and signed up his new act for the hottest talent showcase in America, *The Ed Sullivan Show.*

Sullivan, a newspaper gossip columnist, had been chosen to host a TV variety show because he had no talent or personality himself and thus would never outshine any of the performers. Though he couldn't remember his guests' names, was subject to bizarre tics, and recently had been pronounced clinically dead by a team of top physicians from Johns Hopkins University, Sullivan was a shrewd judge of talent and upon hearing Elvis in rehearsal, told him, "You'll go far, you cute little Italian mouse, but I want you to think about changing your name to Topo Gigio."

Elvis was an immediate sensation. With his sensuous upper lip curling, his axle-greased hair falling over his sweaty chin, and his lust-filled voice yearning hungrily for hound dogs and blue suede

---

1. Colonel Parker died in 1983 at the age of 147, after admitting to Elvis biographer Arthur Schlesinger Jr. that he had slipped LSD into Phillips's coffee, causing Phillips's judgment to suffer during the game.

shoes, Elvis electrified the nation. The wiring took forever but it was worth it. People were really shocked. The triumph came even though Sullivan (worried about complaints from the Catholic Anti-Penis League) ordered the cameramen not to show Elvis's most charismatic feature, his groin, which gyrated so wildly that at one point, it knocked down a performing bear rehearsing backstage.[2] Sullivan also had the studio audience blindfolded but one woman peeked and was transformed into a pillar of salt.

After being drafted into the Army and accidentally starting the Vietnam war, Elvis returned home to wed his teenage sweetheart, Priscilla Boogaloo, first having her tested to make sure that she was a virgin and changed her panties daily. Despite his intense fabulousness, Elvis did have his peculiarities. "Ah like sex," he told reporters on returning from his honeymoon. "It's real good, especially when you take your pants off first."

But when his naïve young bride discovered that Elvis refused to give up his other girlfriends and kept four of them in the basement of their home even after the marriage, Priscilla left him, taking their baby daughter, Anastasia.[3] Heartbroken, Elvis retired from show business and grew obese, prophesying, "Without my moral guidance, that po' little girl of mine is in danger of growing up to marry the weirdest man in America."

Unable to go to the park and nap on benches like a normal vagrant for fear of setting off riots, Elvis had nothing to do but sit around his new mansion, which he had bought from a rich Memphis widow named Grace Land. There, he passed the time

2. Upon regaining consciousness, the bear proposed to Elvis and became so aroused it had to be subdued by six security guards.

3. Who emerged from seclusion years later as Britney Spears after a worldwide search for Elvis's missing daughter, conducted by the *National Enquirer*.

Two Different Countries

What was America like in the days when the young Elvis emerged from obscurity to transform music and all human life forever? Many Americans are too young to remember how different things were back in the '50s. Many other Americans are too old to remember. Here are the facts as compiled by a panel of prominent historians:

Then: Teenagers in hot rods terrorized their communities.

Now: Adults in SUVs terrorize their communities.

Now: People communicate through cell phones, e-mail, pagers.

Then: People communicated by yelling at each other.

Then: Everyone expected to do hard manual labor throughout lives, then die at early age.

Now: Everyone expects to become a star, get rich, have constant sex with younger people, and avoid work.

Then: Sex illegal except between consenting farm animals.

Now: Sex open to people of all ages.

Then: Old people desperately unhip.

Now: Old people get new hips.

Now: Sophisticated charts, top-ten lists, colorful graphics convey information.

Then: People could read.

Now: Rock and roll free to express any idea in any style.

Then: Rock and roll good.

Following his daily sex workout, the ever-considerate Elvis takes the trouble to rate his partner's performance, pointing out areas where it could be improved, even though he will never see her again.

with his favorite hobbies: shooting at television sets with a pistol, eating sandwiches the size of a sofa, burping, having sex with floozies brought in by his loyal "Memphis Mafia" (a loose-knit gang of good ol' Sicilians who had earned his loyalty by killing enemies for him), and testing experimental medications for the nation's major pharmaceutical companies.

Nine years later, bored and cranky, Elvis made a spectacular comeback, traveling to Las Vegas, where he filmed the TV special, *Bored and Cranky, Elvis Makes a Spectacular Comeback*. Now he was bigger than ever (well over 500 pounds, in fact) and soon had broken every show-biz record ever set.

Having achieved everything achievable, Elvis had no choice but to drop dead, which he did on August 16, 1977. Though his old friend Ed Sullivan had made a deal with Colonel Parker to show the death live on stage, Elvis, impulsive to the end, was unable to get to the studio in time.

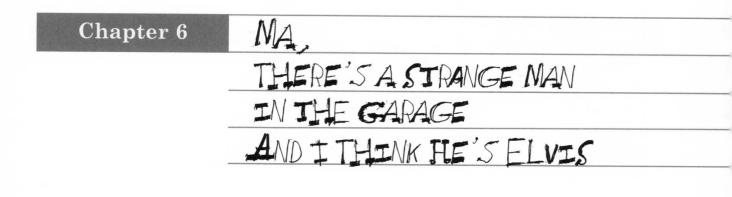

Chapter 6

MA,
THERE'S A STRANGE MAN
IN THE GARAGE
AND I THINK HE'S ELVIS

After his demise, Elvis refused to remain confined in his sequined white marble tomb in Memphis's famed Dead Rock Star Cemetery as a typical, unamazing corpse would. This was so Elvis of him. Just as he had rebelled against the boring popular music of the '50s when he burst out of nowhere with his raw "rockabilly" sound and his illegal hips, he now rebelled against the boring tradition of lying quietly in the coffin and not making a fuss.

Instead he went on his greatest personal appearance tour.

People began spotting Elvis all over America, at truck stops and diners, in the alleys behind Greek coffee shops, lurking near the dumpster in the parking lot of Kentucky Fried Chicken franchises, even in the shadowy wine cellars of upscale gourmet restaurants. It seemed that wherever it was possible to snag a doughnut, a hamburger, or a loose escargot, Elvis was there, a beacon of hope to the hungry, the thirsty, and the soon-to-be-dead.

Soon reports were also coming in from farmers and backpackers in remote regions that Elvis had been seen emerging from vehicles piloted by extraterrestrial beings and describing interesting trips he had taken to planets in far-off galaxies.

The Brain
Beneath
the Crown

People who did not know Elvis personally often ask the question, "Wasn't he really kind of a moron?" To lay to rest his own doubts regarding his intelligence, Elvis bequeathed his head to the University of Miami's Department of Forensic Brainology for study. (His only proviso was that it not be removed before his death.) After eight years of intense study, including the division of the brain into three sections (left brain, right brain, and bizarre, six-pound, still-pulsating tumor), Miami's research team concluded that "Yes, actually, Elvis really was kind of a moron."

Meanwhile, thousands of Elvis impersonators of every race, gender, and height appeared and began stalking the landscape, singing all of Elvis's hits. One of them, Alan Greenspan, eventually became chairman of the Federal Reserve, the most powerful nonmusical position in America.

It soon became evident to Americans, a very religious people, that the only possible explanation for all this was that Elvis was divine. The First Church of Elvis was founded and Elvisism became one of the world's major religions. Millions of pilgrims trek to the Grace Land shrine every year to pray, meditate, and purchase holy relics such as Elvis T-shirts, coffee mugs, syringes, and lawn ornaments.

As for Elvis himself, he now sits at God's side and rules over all of North America, and as far south as Nicaragua. It should surprise no one to learn that the Supreme Being is a major fan and has every one of Elvis's albums, though *Viva Las Vegas* is his favorite.

Awed mechanics try to touch the car of the risen Elvis as the dead rock icon drives through a Detroit auto-body shop in a 1997 sighting.

Chapter 7

THE ROCKING, ROLLING, ROLLICKING, AND FOL-DE-ROLING OF AMERICA

Now the rock was on a roll. All over the nation (and in parts of Arkansas as well) it blared from radios, record players, bars, high-school gyms, maximum-security penal institutions, and fire engines, although the last may have just been the sirens, come to think of it. Everywhere, tired feet perked up to the sound and danced to the frenzied, irresistible beat, even though their panicky owners often tried to stop them.

Once Elvis had shown that white people had rhythm—at least a few of them—new stars popped up everywhere, which is why they were called pop stars.

Jerry Lee Lewis, a wild-eyed Southerner with flying yellow hair, pounded on his piano keys, whooped, yelped, and occasionally even sang, driving audiences into delirium with hits like "Great Balls of Fire," which told the story of an Italian restaurant notorious for using too much spice, and "Whole Lotta Shakin' Goin' On," a song about Parkinson's disease.[1] Starting out as a comedian in Tupelo, Mississippi, he had split with his partner, crooner Dean Lee Martin, and turned to rock and roll because it was funnier than comedy. Lewis made the most of his talent for zany slapstick, climbing atop the piano and playing it with his toes, nose, tongue, and some body parts you wouldn't believe.

Buddy Holly was a goofy-looking young man with big horn-rimmed glasses and even bigger teeth who wrote and performed a string of bright, bouncy hits with his group of tiny, six-legged musicians, the Crickets. It was Holly who invented the verbal "hiccup," a technique enabling a singer to incorporate esophageal reflux into his music, which added a nutritional dimension to rock and roll and was later

---

1. Though the song achieves a rhythmic intensity of near-earthquake proportions, the author cannot condone its cruel and offensive lyrics.

adopted by Meat Loaf, the Platters, Milli Vanilli and other food-oriented rockers. (At the time of his tragic death, Buddy was working on the burp. Had he lived long enough to complete it, there is no telling how far his digestion might have taken this seminal figure.) As a lyricist, Holly brought a new complexity to the form. His growing sophistication emerged in songs like the evocative "Peggy Sue":

> *Peggy Sue*
> *Peggy Sue*
> *Pretty pretty pretty pretty*
> *Peggy Sue*
> *Oh, Peggy*
> *My Peggy Sue-hoo-hoo*
> *Well, I love you, gal*
> *And I want you, Peggy Sue[2]*

Johnny Cash, whose voice was incredibly expressive for someone with a two-note range, couldn't decide whether to sing rock and roll or country, so he sang rockabilly, a combination of rock and billy. Always dressed in black, he could not be seen outdoors at night and eventually was hit by a car while strolling down the middle of a highway, his favorite section. But he used the experience to his advantage, writing one of his biggest hits, "I Walk the Line."

Another rockabillyist, Carl Perkins, had always been obsessed with footgear and cleanliness, so it was only natural for him to

Candid shot of Buddy Holly and his Crickets relaxing backstage in an unguarded moment.

2. Lyrics reprinted by permission of Peggy Sue.

combine the two. He came up with the rock classic "Blue Suede Shoes," with its haunting theme of a man's need to preserve his nap against all odds in a world that loves to scuff. When Perkins sang, "You can do anything, but lay offa my blue suede shoes," you could feel the angst of not just his lonely, tender feet but all sad feet everywhere. Some rock and rollers had soul; Carl Perkins had sole. Doubtless he would have been a far greater figure in rock and roll history, but when Elvis recorded the song and sold more records than Perkins did with his own version, Perkins developed an impacted bunion and was never the same.

The Everly Brothers, two brothers named Everly, woke up a sleeping nation (though which nation has never been disclosed) with "Wake Up, Little Susie." Schoolchildren identified with this amusing ditty in which a young boy tries desperately to revive his sister after accidentally strangling her.

Ray Charles blended gospel, blues, R&B, and Braille into early rock classics such as "What'd I Say?"—a musical complaint in which he protests that he can't hear his own singing over the loud music of his band.

Willie Clyde Puckett was the first performer to attempt combining rockabilly and classical music. Born in Chattahoochee, Florida, the son of a turnip farmer and a Juilliard-trained violinist, he struck gold with his first record, "I Ain't Got No Money, Honey (I'm as Baroque as You)." Playing a mean electric cello and backed up by his Wolf Gang, Puckett might have been one of the near-greats had he not died tragically of an overdose of snuff just before a hootenanny at Carnegie Hall.

The Six Life of the Early Rockers

It's been said that there are only twelve plots in all fiction. Or is it fifteen? No matter. It's much the same with the rock and roll of the '50s and '60s. Nearly every song revolves around one of just six basic themes:

1. I love you and I will always love you no matter what may happen, even death or growing up. (Mainly because you are really cute.)

2. I love you but you don't love me and thus I am very, very unhappy.

3. I want to do it with you. Please let me. It would make me very, very happy.

4. You and I will do it tonight, I'm pretty sure, and then I will be very, very, happy. Ecstatic, really.

5. Not only are you not doing it with me but I suspect you are doing it with someone else and thus I am very, very unhappy. Miserable, in fact.

6. I had you but you left me, and now I'm so very, very unhappy I feel like I wanna die.

Chapter 8

ON THE PROTEAN REFULGENCE OF ROY ORBISON

by Guest Author
William F. Buckley Jr.[1]

ROY IS SO COOL

A Simultaneous Translation

by James T. Winsloop III,
Daily News Digest Writer for
President George W. Bush

It was in the Fall of 1990 that, thanks to a contretemps involving a bibulous chauffeur, I found myself patronizing a cinematic venue for the first time in several decades. Sojourning to Hartford, Connecticut, to deliver a discourse entitled "Just What Was So Exploitive About Slavery, Anyway?" before an audience of retired howitzer manufacturers, I instead fetched up at the Sunshine Cineplex in Sarasota, Florida. Fortunately, I was able to complete two espionage novels and the fourth book of my nine-volume biography of Friedrich Hayek in the backseat while the malign inebriate at the con divagated through the Interstate Highway System.

---

1. Mr. Buckley is the first of several distinguished writers who have graciously consented, sometimes as a result of blackmail or physical threats, to contribute a chapter to this book. In addition to his other diverse interests, he is an authority on the subject of Roy Orbison, a giant of early rock and roll.

I went to a flick a few years back. Some drunk got me in trouble so I hid in there.

Anyway, I got my first peek at Julia Roberts. Wow! What a babe. I've really got a thing for her now.

That song got to me, too. You know, "Pretty Woman." So I was like, Whoa, get me everything by Roy Orbison.

His progress was finally halted outside the Sunshine but not before he had annihilated a family of three who were attempting to traverse an intersection. This left me little choice but to debouch from the limo and seek sanctuary within the cinema lest the paparazzi and tabloid quidnuncs, with their preternatural aptitude for ferreting out the spoor of the illustrious, materialize and bring gratuitous opprobrium upon your blameless correspondent.

Purchasing a ducat, I settled into the crepuscular murk, managing to dash off an essay or two by penlight while some brummagem entitled *Pretty Woman* unfolded onscreen. After composing a typically scintillating Buckleyism comparing President George H.W. Bush's disposition to that of St. Augustine, I chanced to look up and succumbed to unanticipated infatuation upon observing the callipygian pulchritude of Miss Roberts, so much so that I resolved on the spot to work her into rotation with Miss Crawford, my onanistic fantasy inamorata since puberty. (Nor have I ever had cause to regret my impulsive decision. Miss Roberts is *transcendent*.)

I lingered to scrutinize the film four more times, then left humming the title song, which, however unbidden, had mysteriously subjugated and colonized my consciousness. Returning home, I dispatched myriad assistants to investigate the provenance of this opus and was presently informed it had been composed and recorded by a Mr. Roy Orbison. Unhappily, I had never heard of this prodigy, having confined my musical peregrinations to "The Three Bs," i.e., Herr Bach, Herr Beethoven, and Mr. Benny Goodman, a woodwind nonpareil of Hebraic extraction.

Suffice it to say that Mr. Orbison became an obsession. By degrees, I procured the entirety of his oeuvre and, committing prodigious quantities to memory, endeavored to play it on my harpsichord. Subsequently, when perorating on the malevolence of liberalism to groveling interns at the *National Review* or lunching with corporate panjandrums at the Yale Club, I confess I often found myself crooning "dum dum dum dumby doo wah" simply for the sheer rapture of the exercise. You may imagine the consternation this engendered, to say nothing of the sussurus of senility intimated by my manifold nemeses.

It was not merely the dazzling crescendos of Mr. Orbison's plummy yet ethereal voice, with its three-octave range, or the impassioned melodrama of his plangent lyrics that so impinged upon my psyche, but the uncanny way in which his works somehow recapitulated the excruciating angst of my own adolescence, which I had suppressed for many long decades, though admittedly at the cost of my immortal soul. To obscure my deep-seated neuroses, I had projected an Olympian persona and gradually evolved into the tumid, reactionary apologist for the worst excesses of the wealthy and powerful who is so venerated by the vacuous and the misanthropic. But please disregard, for the nonce, my personal trauma; I shall expound fully on that theme in a forthcoming atonement for my squandered talent, *Wrong to be Right*. This piece is not about my iniquities but rather the genius of a dazzling virtuoso.

And it is only when we contemplate his magnum opus, "Oh, Pretty Woman" (for such is its formal cognomen), that paean to sequestration redeemed, that we absorb the quintessence of the

Damn, Roy was one fine, kick-ass singer. He kind of took me back to my youth. I was pretty screwed up then. I decided, hell, I'll act all hoity-toity so nobody knows what a dork I am. I guess it stuck.

Thing about "Pretty Woman," though, is if you really listen to it, it's not just some dumb song. There's a message!

Orbison style. "Pretty woman, walking down the street," he begins in a passage of deceptive simplicity. For we soon realize that this is no ordinary female but an idealized vision of all womanhood, the eternal locus of male desire, or, in Mr. Orbison's delicate aperçu, "the kind I'd like to meet." Such is her flawlessness that her reality must at first be denied: "I don't believe you, you're not the truth. No one could look as good as you."

But this vain attempt at self-deception is immediately dashed by a cathartic outburst of pure emotional veracity that will brook no resistance. "Mercy!" ejaculates the singer. His pathetic attempt to extrude a testaceous husk around his wounded psyche has been obliterated by the puissance of the Pretty Woman's animal magnetism and now he is devastated by the realization that he, a gauche, proletarian autodidact sans Ivy League diploma or Swiss chalet, will never gain the opportunity to—in the vulgar argot of the "street," which I have always detested with every fiber of my patrician being but which (let us be scrupulous) occasionally bestows upon us the pluperfect idiom—fuck her.

See, the guy in the song is down on himself. He thinks he doesn't deserve this hottie who's walking down the street. He's all, "Oh, please! Don't make me cry!" Jeez, what a wuss.

Roy Orbison in a scene from his first (and only) movie, a Western titled *Fastest Guitar in the West*. Roy starred as a singing outlaw whose use of a gun hidden in a guitar succeeded until he met a sheriff with a tuba-propelled grenade.

There follows more frustration, more beseeching: "Pretty woman, don't walk on by. Pretty woman, don't make me cry," our lachrymose narrator pules. But then, just as he is prepared to capitulate and retreat to his abysmal anchoritic existence... *mirabile dictu!*

> *What do I see?*
> *Is she walking back to me?*
> *Yes, she's walking back to me!*

A metamorphosis has eventuated. The pretty woman's epiphany, her sudden recognition of the supplicant's merit despite his phthisic appearance, validates his suffering and brings him (as well as us) beatitude. Surely a lesser artist would not have dared to attempt such a bravura culmination, would have dismissed it as bathetic tripe. It is the refulgence of Mr. Orbison that he rejects such superficial temporizing and instead allows us to savor a serendipitous lagniappe.

"Oh," he cries in ecstasy. "Oh, pretty woman." And with this incantation, his fissured heart is reconstituted and his *Weltschmerz* atomized, and ours as well. Finally, it can be said, one has achieved termination of one's exegesis and now one awaits with roseate anticipation one's pecuniary reward, that munificent recompense which was, to be sure, one's sole incentive for contriving this euphuistic cockalorum.

But guess what...it turns out the chick digs him!

Which just goes to prove that even if the whole world thinks you're doing something stupid, you've gotta stick to your guns! See it through! Stay the course!

Song Titles Rejected By Roy Orbison Before Settling on "Pretty Woman"

1. Gorgeous Female
2. 'Tractive Girlie
3. Lovely Lady
4. Fem'nine Cutie
5. Winsome Charmer
6. Sexy Baby
7. Petite Poontang
8. Charming Pinup
9. Scary Mantrap
10. Witchy Sorc'ress
11. Mousy Waitress
12. Unsightly Harlot

Chapter Titles Rejected By William F. Buckley Jr. Before Settling on "On the Protean Refulgence of Roy Orbison"

1. RO: An Overview
2. The Most Unforgettable Character I Ever Met
3. Some Improvisations on an Orbisonian Theme
4. *Ad Majorem Orbisonis Gloriam*
5. Upon the Inception of an Orbison Esthetic
6. From Telemann to Orbison
7. A Funny Thing Happened to Me on the Way to the Speech

Chapter 9

WHAT ROCKS UP MUST ROLL DOWN

Not everyone loved rock and roll. By the late 1950s, the enemies of this fresh, vibrant new music had coalesced into a stale, boring old conspiracy whose evil tentacles slithered throughout the nation, threatening to choke the life out of rock and roll while it still lay in its crib. (Literally!) They would have acted even earlier but they had to wait for rock and roll to be invented first.

Among the vile plotters of this scheming cabal were politicians, clergymen, leaders of the established music industry, and the usual rich, old, powerful white men who have nothing better to do than sit around trying to squelch anything new and fun that comes along. It's their hobby. Maybe it wouldn't do for you or me but they enjoy it and it keeps them spry so let's not be too quick to judge harshly. Still, if you know one of these rich, old, powerful white men personally, try, if at all possible, to slip some arsenic into his mush when he's not looking.

Rock and roll was attacked on the floor of Congress, as well as on the ceiling, where Representative Harley Clegg of Utah hung from a trapeze as he called it "a Communist plot to turn our children into sexed-up monkey boys who fornicate in public with their own moms and then sit around afterward making smart-aleck remarks and drinking beer, not decent domestic brands but subversive, imported foreign beer." The Reverend Billy Graham said it was "Satan's favorite music, I'm sure, though personally, I've never heard any myself." Even Frank Sinatra denounced rock and roll, calling it "scoobie-doobie-doodoo."

Rock-and-roll records were burned in public ceremonies in the north and hanged in the south. Many cities banned rock-and-roll concerts. Idaho, taking no chances, banned all music of any kind.

A stick-brandishing anti-rock mob works itself into a frothing rage in Fleckston, Idaho. Minutes later, it went berserk and trampled a Carl Perkins record to death.

Not to be outdone, North Dakota banned Idaho. M. Bubba Thornton Jr. III, a lawyer and leading citizen of Mobile, Alabama, moved his family to England because it was "a God-fearing, civilized country where this degenerate rock-and-roll garbage will never catch on."

The "payrolla" scandal drove another arrow into the pulsing groin of rock and roll. "Ouch!" said rock and roll. Authorities discovered that disc jockeys were taking money from their employers to play rock-and-roll records on the radio instead of working for the sheer joy of it. It was terribly disillusioning for their trusting listeners, and it gave the newspapers yet another opportunity to run banner headlines reading:

ROCK AND ROLL VERY BAD!

The low point (only one foot above sea level) came on February 3, 1959. In a driving snowstorm outside Snard, Iowa, a small U-Haul rental plane took off after a rock concert at a local convenience store. Aboard were the 22-year-old Buddy Holly and two other bright young rock stars, Richie Valens and the Big Bopper (real name: John T. Bigbopper). They had just completed a wildly successful appearance before seven screaming teenagers and were heading for the next stop in their tour, a Sunoco gas station near Lincoln, Nebraska.

They never arrived.[1]

As the plane lifted off the runway, the engine sputtered, then quit, and the aircraft banked sharply into a grove of birch trees on a slight rise near a bend in a river below a hill next to a highway

1. When you see a three-word paragraph like this, you know something *really* dramatic is coming next.

over a ravine beside a bridge. A loud bang was heard as well as the sickening crumpling of metal. Everyone aboard was dead,[2] a condition radically different from the one they'd been in moments before. No one saw the two murky men who melted into the woods, carrying a poison-tipped bazooka. The anti-rock conspiracy had struck another deadly blow.[3]

A wave of shocked disbelief quickly spread among the performers and fans of rock and roll, drowning several. After all, it must be remembered that these were the first major rock-and-roll deaths and no one was prepared for them. The teenagers of America had never had the facts of death explained to them, most parents then believing that their offspring should not learn of the inescapable doom facing every human being until at least 30 years of age, lest they turn permanently melancholy. A veritable pall—which is a bit thicker than veritable haze but not as smoky as veritable smog—seemed to settle over the nation.

Thirteen years later, in 1972, the folksinger Don McLean eloquently captured the dark mood of that moment in his hit "American Pie." With its haunting lyrics that spoke so movingly of Southern good ol' boys driving their Chevys to the levee where they drank whiskey and rye, McLean's song brilliantly caught the spirit of Buddy Holly and his wintry death in a plane in the Midwest. Indeed, it was, as McLean so aptly put it, "the day the music got sick and coughed up some phlegm and had to go lie down for a while." (Later, he was persuaded by his record company to change the line to the less interesting but more commercial "the day the music died.")

---

2. Except for one man, the rock-and-roll singer Tiny Tim. He was never the same after the crash. The trauma changed him into a tall, neurotic geek who from then on sang 50-year-old ballads in a quavering soprano.

3. I have in my possession the documents that unquestionably prove the veracity of this charge. Fifty years after my death, the sealed evidence will be made available to scholars and the full story will finally be known.

Chapter 10

ZOMBIES DANCE ON BUDDY'S GRAVE

The fatal "crash" in Iowa was merely stage one of the nefarious machinations of the insidious cabal. (Or, for those of you lacking Mr. Buckley's vocabulary, the nasty doings of the bad guys.)

One by one, all the real rock stars began to disappear. As noted earlier (and I hope you were paying attention because the material gets a lot harder now and if you weren't you'll be completely lost), Chuck Berry was tossed in jail. Little Richard became a minister, an even harsher punishment. Elvis was drafted and when he returned from the Army, he was no longer the sneering, pelvic savage of yore (or mine, for that matter) but an oddly docile fellow crooning "Love Me Tender" to Hollywood starlets in bland movies. (Of course, he did have sex with them all—Colonel Parker put that in Elvis's contract—but he was not allowed to do this onscreen.) And Jerry Lee Lewis's career was destroyed when he was accused of marrying his 13-year-old cousin. (Of course, he did marry his 13-year-old cousin, but at the time, so had about 76 percent of Southern males, so how was Jerry Lee to know there was anything wrong with it?)

Obviously, it was the antirock conspiracy behind all these disasters. We know this now because we've become much smarter. At the time, no one suspected a thing. What fools we were!

Someone was needed to replace the fallen idols. The public had tasted rock stars, enjoyed the flavor and, like Oliver Twist with his gruel, begged for more, only this time with raisins.[1] The conspiracy was ready. The Era of the Rock Zombies was about to dawn.

---

1. Even I don't fully understand this metaphor but you have to admit, it has a certain resonance.

Actress Ann-Margret marvels at the incredibly lifelike appearance of Pat Boone.

One of the northern bastions of rock and roll in the '50s was Philadelphia. There a disc jockey, a mannish-looking boy calling himself Dick Clark (real name: Richard Clark), had discovered that rock and roll could be televised five days a week, apparently without any lingering medicinal aftertaste. His crude but sophisticated stratagem was to have performers pretend to sing their recorded hits (a technique known as lip-syncing) while local teenagers, dragooned by press gangs from local teen hangouts where they'd been slipped knockout drops, pretended to dance (a technique known as hip-syncing).

American Bandstand was a hit in Philadelphia, won a network slot, and proved to be a national success. Every afternoon, teenage girls across the U.S. rushed home from school and did their homework while their mothers watched Dick Clark, dancing around the living room and wishing their husbands were more communicative and sensitive to their needs, although that had nothing to do with rock and roll. (I just tossed that in to add some pathos.)

With his "hep" teen expressions, such as "I'm gonna play a really good song now," his pleasant little face, and his bland manner—behind which lurked the brain of a really boring businessman—Dick Clark went on to found and acquire record companies and related businesses until he owned 93 percent of the rock-and-roll industry. Then, capping a fabulous career, he was appointed by President Gerald Ford as Official Greeter of New Year's Eve, a lifetime position especially created to make use of Clark's unique broadcasting talents, although no one has ever figured out exactly what they are. (Clark would remain in the post throughout the

1990s, even though by then, being over 100 years old, he was actually being face-synced by a younger man.)

Among the performers turning up on *Bandstand* were incredibly realistic human replicas with typical American names like Frankie, Bobby, and Fabian. They looked like rock stars. They moved like rock stars. They copulated with their teenage fans like rock stars. The only thing they didn't do like rock stars was *rock*. What came out of their mouths wasn't really rock and roll. It was a watered-down, cleaned-up facsimile. It was tame, it was lame, it was a crying shame. It was bland, it was canned, it was...well, you get the picture.

Manufactured in a secret assembly plant whose exact location was known only to the conspiracy, the pseudo-rock creatures were infiltrated into the Clark show.[2] But they were mere prototypes. Even as they went into action, the veiled masterminds of the conspiracy were perfecting a new and more efficient model. They dressed it in a cute sweater and even cuter white buck shoes and unleashed it on a defenseless teenage populace.

Its name was Pat Boone. It was so clean-cut, decent, and just plain nice, you could vomit. (But please, not on my book!)

Boone, who claimed to be a descendant of frontier hero Daniel Boone[3] and his wife Debby, recorded his own versions of all 6,439 rock songs then in existence. No one could stop him. Anyone who

THIRTEEN GREAT
HISTORICAL FIGURES
WHO WOULD HAVE BEEN
ROCKERS
HAD THEY BEEN BORN
LATER

1. King Arthur *(heavy metal)*
2. Rasputin *(gospel)*
3. Billy the Kid *(rockabilly)*
4. Chopin *(art rock)*
5. Nero *(punk)*
6. Frederick Douglass *(soul/funk)*
7. Rudolph Valentino *(glam/glitter)*
8. Oscar Wilde *(rap)*
9. Benito Mussolini *(shock metal)*
10. Isadora Duncan *(disco)*
11. Walt Whitman *(folk rock)*
12. Rimbaud *(acid rock)*
13. Picasso *(blues)*

2. An international tribunal called by the United Nations in Vienna in 1996 to investigate crimes against popular culture cleared Dick Clark of any guilt in the atrocity, accepting his tearful plea that he been used as a dupe by powerful forces he did not understand and could not possibly be the secret mastermind behind the Conspiracy because "he just looks like too nice a guy."

3. Daniel Boone was the subject of many frontier legends, including one that he killed a full-grown bear by breathing in its face after a lunch of pickled pig's feet cooked in garlic sauce. Still, it was Davy Crockett who got a hit song written about him. Go figure.

tried soon found himself blackballed from watching the Miss America Pageant on television or receiving the *Saturday Evening Post* in the mail. Such was the power of the conspiracy.

Boone's music had its roots in the raw, agonized wail of the minuet and the blunt sexual anger of Lawrence Welk.[4] His backup group, the Covers, blasted out a cascade of surging, savage sound with amped-up accordions, banjos, kazoos, and glockenspiels.

The lyrics were reworked for maximum mojo (love that word!) with minimal double entendre. Where Fats Domino had sung "Ain't That a Shame," Pat Boone recorded "Isn't That an Egregious Embarrassment." The Elvis hit "All Shook Up" became "Greatly Agitated." Jerry Lee Lewis's "Whole Lotta Shakin' Goin' On" was transformed to the catchy "Abundance of Vibration Occurring." Big Bill Broonzy's suggestive R&B classic "I'm Gonna Jump on Yo' Big Beautiful Butt and Hump Away All Night" was cleverly changed into "Love Letters in the Sand."

Boone pumped out hundreds of hit records, made numerous movies and starred in a television series before he suffered a transmission failure and was scrapped, his parts cannibalized and recycled to fabricate Paul Anka, Engelbert Humperdinck, and Michael Bolton.

4. A late-twentieth-century bandleader thought to be addicted to champagne. He featured the singing group the Lennon Sisters, whose gentle harmonies so inspired future Beatle John Lennon that he named himself after them.

Chapter 11

THE DARKNESS JUST BEFORE THE GLOOM

As the 1950s gave way to the 1960s—not that anyone noticed—the world of pop and rock frantically thrashed about, trying to rediscover the path to lost glory, as well as to the bathroom, which had also unaccountably been mislaid, probably just off the path to lost glory. A dynamic young president, John F. Kennedy, succeeded the old war hero Dwight D. Eisenhower in the White House and though warned by the FBI (as it had warned every president since Grover Cleveland) that rock and roll was a Communist plot, JFK was known to have expressed curiosity about it, often asking his brother, Bobby, "Do you think Elvis gets more girls than I do?"

The music business, with sales of records and black leather jackets booming, had suddenly exploded into a major industry, wounding hundreds of bystanders. All it needed now was some music. Because the U.S. was (and by some accounts still is) a large country with an exciting variety of weird and inexplicable tastes, the manufactured stars foisted on America by the Conspiracy could not please everyone. Teenagers in particular had developed an endless craving for new trends to alleviate the boredom of living with their tedious parents. The growing music industry would try to supply them. Among the major trends that blossomed were the ones following this colon:

Doo-Wop

The first doo-wop song was written by Stephen Foster, the only composer of note (or, more accurately, notes) America was able to produce until it came up with March King John Philip Sousa, who wasn't bad in April or May, either. Called "Camptown Races," the Foster tune included the cheerful refrain of "doo-dah, doo-dah," which was misunderstood by many and heard as "doo-wop, doo-wop." Nothing Foster did could convince people to rectify the mistake and he died a broken man, penniless and addicted to camphor balls.

In the early and middle '50s, groups of urban teenagers all over the country—mostly males who weren't tough enough to get into gangs—began gathering on street corners to vocalize, although a few of them preferred to sing. In some neighborhoods, there was a doo-wop group on every street corner, keeping enraged residents up all night with their rowdy harmonizing. Pitched battles often broke out between the two sides, resulting in the singers going off pitch.

Typically, the groups consisted of one boy with a voice, known as the lead singer, and between three and forty others who were called "the jerks in the background." Jealous, the jerks would try to distract the lead singer by chanting silly phrases such as "sh-boom, sh-boom, ya da da da da da da da da da" or "sha na na na na, sha na na na" or "oom papa oom papa mow" or "yo yo ma, yo yo ma, yo' mama got ma yoyo" or "hello, Dolly, well, hello, Dolly, it's so nice to have you back where you belong." If the lead singer allowed himself to become confused and blew his lines, he would be savagely beaten and replaced by one of the jerks.

Inevitably, if not unavoidably, some of the better groups caught the attention of record producers, who were always prowling the streets searching for the latest trend. As the hits started coming, young and barely formed doo-wop groups, some not yet toilet-trained, would be snatched off their street corners, mercilessly shoved into recording studios, and forced to become millionaire pop stars against their will.

One of the greatest flashes in the pan of the period, Joey Acapella, lead singer of Joey and the Smirkers, remembers what it was like:

> Me and the boys, we was grabbed right out of metal shop at Industrial
> Mechanics High. Jerry Minkney from Decca come into the classroom and
> took us at gunpoint. He told me, "You'll sing. You'll sing like a canary,
> you little son of a bitch, if you know what's good for you." I didn't want
> to sing but I was scared.

At first, all the doo-woppers, as they were seldom called, named themselves after birds (the Ravens, the Orioles, the Penguins, the Flamingos, the Finches, the Dodos, the Cassowaries, the Ibises, the Red-Tufted Nuthatches). Later, though, they switched to cars (the Cadillacs, the El Dorados, the Edsels, the Mazdas, the Humvees, the Valiants, the Studebakers, the Jeep Grand Cherokees). All this culminated with the greatest of all doo-wop groups, the Buick Skylarks. Later groups tried cereals (the Cheerios, the Wheaties, the Farinas, the Post Toasties, the Raisin Brans) and then mattresses (the Sertas, the Sealy Posturepedics, the Beautyrests, the Sagging Lumpys), but it just didn't work. They had run out of good names and doo-wop was over.

Girl Groups

The girl groups (sometimes spelled "gurl groops") were completely different from the doo-wop groups in that they were not boys. Why those singing soft rock felt the need to divide according to sex is not clear, though some anthropologists believe it was a custom that spilled over from high-school gym classes.

While the doo-wop groups were forming on street corners, the girl groups assembled in ladies' rest rooms, which explains why there were so many of them: fewer of the girls died from exposure to the elements.[1] Another crucial difference was that instead of singing "doo-wop, doo-wop," the backup singers of the girl groups sang "da doo ron ron ron, da doo ron ron."

This chorus derived from the Da Doos' unforgettable classic "Da Doo Ron Ron," about a very confused girl, who sang:

> *I met him on a Sunday and my heart stood still*
>
> *My girlfriend told me that his name was Bill*
>
> *But I never liked that name*
>
> *Which explains why I'm not singing*
>
> *Da Doo Bill Bill Bill*
>
> *Da Doo Bill Bill*

---

1. Though there were exceptions, such as the Ronettes, several of whom expired shortly after recording their hit "Walking in the Rain."

'Twas Brillig

Located near Times Square on New York's fabled Tin Pan Alley, just east of Copper Pot Place, the Brill Building was erected in 1906 by wealthy industrialist Balthazar Brill, known as the Copper King for his practice of bribing police officials to look the other way as he forced employees to pay him for the privilege of working in his mines and factories. But in the early '60s, it was reborn as a hit factory, its ten sweaty stories teeming with starving teenaged songwriters, all banging away on pianos in vast, noisy rooms without walls. Only the deafest could survive in such a competitive environment. "It was so exciting," recalls Neil Sedaka, who was born in Brooklyn, only a half-hour subway ride away. "I wish I had been there." The Brill Building. Another great building in the history of rock and roll.

Most of the girl-group songs were about boys, except for those like "Leader of the Pack" by the Shangri-Las, which was about dead boys. Fondly recalled as the first song to employ a motorcycle engine as a musical instrument, it told the heartrending story of the obsessed leader of a biker gang who is killed when, on a rainy day that has made the roads slippery, he tries to ride his Harley indoors only to collide with an ottoman.

Most of the successful girl groups were dominated by powerful record producers who molded their careers and fondled their breasts. The most important producer, Don Kirshner, had an entire building in New York filled with songwriters who did nothing but compose for girl groups. When the girl-group trend ended, he changed it into a garment factory, made the songwriters cut cloth, and became a successful fashion mogul under the name Donna Karan.

Another girl-group producer, Phil Spector, invented the famed Wall of Sound. A perceptive analyst of human psychology, Spector built a wall between the girl singers and the musicians accompanying them, usually all males. That way they could concentrate on the music instead of constantly having sex, thus doubling their productivity.[2]

The Twist

Everyone was looking for a new twist when Hank Ballard, a singer of ballads,[3] found it. It was the Twist. One day, Ballard had just stepped out of the shower, donned his slippers, and begun energetically drying his buttocks with a towel slung between both

---

2. Spector married one of his stars, Ronnie Spector, whom he fell in love with when he learned they had the same name. Later, she divorced him, citing "irreconcilable weirdness."

3. Note: Some sources call him Hank Ballad, a singer of ballards.

hands when he saw a lit cigarette on the floor and stubbed it out with the toe of his right foot. As he looked into the mirror and saw himself, he realized he had invented a new dance. On the spot, he began shouting this fateful plea:

> *Come on, baby,*
> *Let's do the Twist*

But there were no babies in the house so he had to do it by himself. Then he realized he was twisting and shouting, which gave rise to yet another song.

Teenagers do the Plunge, a popular dance of the early '60s, in which one partner would leap off a balcony or staircase and land atop the other, dislocating his neck.

Twist and shout

Someone please get me out

I'm locked in

My damn bathroom

And I've twisted my ankle

Ballard recorded "The Twist," but the version that took off was that of Chubby Checker, a supermarket worker from Philadelphia whose real name was Chubby Chaser.[4] While shopping one day during rush hour, Dick Clark spotted the young man twisting his way down the crowded aisles trying to avoid the lurching, weaving shopping carts. Soon he was twisting on *American Bandstand* and making twisted records.

The Twist swept America[5] and ignited a national dance craze, setting numerous toes on fire. Not just teenagers but even extremely old people (over age 16) twisted the night away at clubs such as the Peppermint Lounge in New York, where Joey Dee and the Deedle-Dee-Dees popularized the Peppermint Twist, although much to their surprise it turned out to be a piece of candy, not a dance.[6]

Ambulances waited outside these new Twist clubs to rush patrons to hospitals to repair their slipped discs and spinal fractures. Everyone from pillars of high society and exemplars of rectitude to rancid lowlife scumbags eventually succumbed to the siren call of the Twist and felt greatly embarrassed when reminded years later how ridiculous they had looked dancing to a siren.

What accounted for the Twist's popularity? There were four factors: 1) Anyone could do it. 2) It could be done by anyone. 3) For the first time, ordinary people, not just black musicians, were allowed to move their hips in public, which was then thought to look wildly sexy and could get one's date all excited. 4) It was so easy to do that virtually any human being could accomplish it.

4. Many people think Chubby Checker's stage name was inspired by Fats Domino, but that is a myth. Actually he modeled himself after the little-known rock sitarist Obese Parcheesi.

5. It was big in England too, where the Royal Family was seen doing it; it therefore became known there as the Twits.

6. It was around this time that the tragically nervous rocker Stocky Scrabble committed suicide when informed that his record, the Twitch, had just missed becoming a national dance craze by a couple of letters.

But the real significance of the Twist was that unlike the other dances of the time, both rock and nonrock, it unleashed the dancer as a totally independent entity. You had a partner but—and this is so significant, I am thinking of putting it in italics; oh, hell, I will put it in italics—*you could pay no attention to her (or him, or them) whatsoever*. In essence, it was every pelvis for itself. This radical departure from all that had gone before in the annals of recorded history led to a surge of rampant individualism which would increase human creativity, enhance personal freedom and autonomy, and essentially spell the end of civilization.[7]

The Twist craze lasted a long time, perhaps twelve or fourteen minutes. Toward the twilight of its dominance, some farsighted men and women and a few who were nearsighted but wore corrective lenses saw that new dances might succeed the Twist and capture similar glory. These visionaries lost no time. In short order, they gave the world the Mashed Potato, the Swim, the Frug, the Watusi, the Pygmy, the Octopus, the Jerk, the Tic, the Thrash, the Cough, the Heave, the Inquisition,[8] and the Fellatio, which later caught on as a nonmusical trend. But there was a problem: all this dancing was making everyone very tired. The effect was soon evident when people began doing the Yawn, the Nap, the Snore, and the Snooze.

Obviously, rock and roll in America was in a state of creative exhaustion. What was desperately needed was something new, something fresh, something different. And not only that but, should it come, a new chapter to put it in. Because this one's much too long already.[9]

It is the end of an era and
Chubby Checker smiles bravely,
but now he is alone. The fickle crowds
have moved on to the Mashed Potato
and here we begin to sense the tragedy
of a man, his hips sore, his ankles
crumbling, a man left slowly twisting
in the wind.

7. Which is spelled like this: t-h-e-e-n-d-o-f-c-i-v-i-l-i-z-a-t-i-o-n.

8. The Inquisition, in which dancers imitated the hideous contortions of a medieval torture victim being disemboweled, drawn, and quartered, was perhaps the least popular of all the popular dance crazes.

9. And has too many footnotes as well.

Chapter 12

THE BRUTISH INVASION

Many young people today ask: Who were the Beatles?

The answer is really quite simple: The Beatles, to put it in terms even a Republican president might understand, were the four greatest human beings who have ever lived since the beginning of mankind's existence on earth.[1]

But we're getting ahead of our story. When we left Chapter 11, as you may recall, things looked dark. But a warming, life-giving sun was about to break through the stormy clouds. The temperature was in the high sixties, a light breeze was blowing from the northwest, and a low-pressure zone was forming over the British Isles. And those very isles, by a bizarre twist of fate no one could have ever predicted,[2] are the exotic setting to which our dramatic tale now shifts! Is this a great true-life adventure saga or what?

You see, England had lost its empire, which meant that its young people, who previously had been shipped off to the colonies to push the natives around, now had nothing to do but bugger about[3] the streets and get in trouble. Naturally, to help accomplish this, they began listening to American rock and roll, even though it was sung in a foreign language.

---

1. Source: Ringo Starr.
2. Except for the legendary seer Nostradamus, who in 1327 prophesied: "In the year following the great sadness, four shaggy minstrels from the damp realm where dwelleth a race of men with bad teeth shall journey to the West and there give voice to a fervent desire to hold your hand. In so doing they shall prosper. But well should they heed this warning: Beware the artsy Japanese chick for she is big, big trouble."
3. Authentic British slang expression of the period, possibly obscene, depending on the pronunciation.

A deranged Mod musician tries to save himself from what he imagines is a mob of fans, but is actually two girls trying to get into a shop to make a purchase.

Thus inspired, the youths divided themselves into two rival gangs, the Mods and the Rockers, so that they could have gang wars. The Rockers wore black leather jackets, rode motorcycles, and sported greasy hair combed like Elvis's, while the Mods favored bowler hats, pink tights, and ballet slippers and rode unicycles while juggling fruit. The Mods were much more creative but the Rockers had tradition on their side, which is always important in England.[3] (The Mods also enjoyed shopping with their "birds" on "swinging Carnaby Street" but that's much too nauseating to go into.)

At first the Mods and Rockers were content with their gang wars, riots, and afternoon teas. But then things took a sinister turn and they began making music. The government became alarmed. As Prime Minister Edward Heath later described it in his memoirs, *The Incredibly Boring Memoirs of Prime Minister Edward Heath*, "The prospect of all that beastly noise ruining our lovely, quiet little country was rather intolerable, really. As a direct result, I became quite irregular in my bowel habits." An emergency meeting of the Cabinet was held and a decision was made not to tell the Queen the bad news for fear she would get that pinched look on her face which spelled so much trouble for Prince Philip and the royal children.

But the official attitude shifted dramatically when the new rock groups began selling so many records that the British economy suddenly threatened to become healthy. Acting boldly, Parliament passed a law taking advantage of the situation, a law that changed

3. A third gang, the Mockers, adopted elements of both the other gangs and tried to make peace between them. For a time they appeared to have succeeded. Unfortunately, however, the Mods and Rockers had only come together in order to wipe out the Mockers.

the course of history: All the British rock groups would be sent to America!

"It was a fiendishly brilliant manoeuvre,"[4] recalls distinguished British rock historian Sir Nick Douglas-Hume-Bennett-Gordon-Pankhurst-Schwartz. "With one stroke, we tapped into the lucrative American market and at the same time rid ourselves of all these annoying troublemakers."

In a series of midnight raids, the police seized thousands of musicians (and their instruments, girl friends, managers, and drug suppliers), drove them to airports, loaded them onto cargo planes, and waved a fond goodbye to the big roaring birds rising like so many flying aircraft into a sky now colored a bright and optimistic blue. This entire throbbing enormity would become known as the Brutish Invasion, and as it streaked inexorably westward, ahead, a trembling, whimpering America sat waiting helplessly, wanting to scream but paralyzed with terror.

There were many great bands in that vast armada, their members dreaming only of meeting their glorious destiny—that is, having sex with as many teenage American girls as possible. But, of course, one band was even more extremely fabulous than the others.

You may have already guessed its name, especially since I just told it to you at the beginning of this chapter. If so, you may now turn the page and read that band's incredible story. If not, you must go back to page one and start all over again. Sorry, but someone has to uphold standards in this sadly degraded time we live in.

4. Actual British spelling.

MOMENTOUS MOMENTS IN ROCK AND ROLL

The Day the Who

Got Smashed

It was the summer of 1964 and the Who (then known as the Why) were playing a grimy pub in the tough, wanking-class town of Rotwich-on-Slimeford before an audience of 500 pill-popping mods and their dates, most of whom were mod models. "It was very dark onstage," recalls Pete Townshend, "and as I whipped into my trademark windmill motion, I accidentally hit bassist John Entwhistle in the face with my guitar." Unruffled, Entwhistle merely smiled and kicked Townshend in the groin. Enraged, Townshend brought his guitar down over Entwhistle's head, which went clear through the instrument. Hearing the wild cheers of the audience, Townshend realized he had created something very exciting. He proceeded to demolish Keith Moon's drum kit, the amps, the microphones, and vocalist Roger Daltrey.

At last the Who were on their way to rock-and-roll immortality.

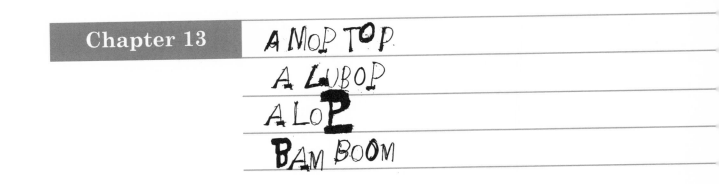

Chapter 13

A MOP TOP
A LUBOP
A LOP
BAM BOOM

The boys who would be known to the world one day as John, Paul, George, and Ringo (at the time, they were too poor to have any names at all) were born between 1940 and 1943 in a blue-collar, brown-shoe, white-sock section of Liverpool called East Tupelo. Liverpool was a port city, which meant that its inhabitants sat around all day drinking port. This explains why nothing of consequence has ever come out of Liverpool before the Beatles or since.

While in high school, John Lennon, the oldest and most rebellious of the four, as well as the one with the longest penis,[1] fell victim to a craze for skiffle music. However, he failed to master the skiffle and quickly switched to guitar. He met Paul McCartney when the two grabbed for the same black leather jacket on sale at a vintage clothing store. (During the scuffle, a rowdy youth named Mick Jagger snatched the jacket, declaring, "Even at this early stage, I am better than you wankers.") Chatting in the ambulance afterwards, they found they both enjoyed Doris Day films, quickly became friends, and decided to found a gang together. After losing 16 consecutive rumbles, a new European record, they realized they needed more members and recruited George Harrison. He was a quiet boy but when he did say something it was usually ignored.

To while away the time between gang wars, the three began playing something amazingly close to music. Two new members then joined. Stu Sutcliffe, an artistic friend of John's, was immensely talented at brooding and considered by many to be the best James Dean impersonator in Liverpool.

1. Source: International Federation of Groupies.

Musically untutored, Sutcliffe at first only pretended to play the guitar, but since four guitars made the band sound unbalanced, he later pretended to play saxophone. Pete Best joined the group after the boys placed a newspaper want ad: "Seeking SWM drummer—must be cool but not too threatening in case we ever want to go big-time. And no smokers!"

At first the group called itself the Quarrymen after their idol, Michelangelo, the greatest rhythm lute player of the Renaissance, who did a little sculpting on the side. But when they couldn't get any gigs[2], they changed the name to the Giggles. That didn't work either so they tried the Five Charming, Tap-Dancing Lads from Liverpool; the Warbling Budgerigars; Herman's Hermits; the Housefly Larvae; the Large Flutterin' Moths That Fly in the Fookin' Window and Flap Frantically around the Light Bulbs; the Beetles; the Silver Beetles; the Dung Beetles; the Volkswagen Beetles; the Bottles; the Beets; and the Meatles. Still no jobs eventuated but the five felt they were on the right track.

Just when their prospects were looking grim enough that the boys were writing out a suicide pact, the government social worker assigned to their case suggested that they go to Germany, where the dreary citizens were so fun-deprived they would welcome even a British rock group that could not play. It was in Hamburg, singing American songs to German audiences in English accents, that the group developed the renowned Beatles sense of humor. Soon they had acquired many fans, which helped them survive the brutal Teutonic summer.

By consuming enormous quantities of German beer, the Beatles, now calling themselves the Beatles (a clever combination of the words "bea" and "tles"), finally worked up the confidence to return to England and become famous. First, they had to fire the hopeless Stu Sutcliffe, who was now pretending to play the pan flute (to soften the blow, they waited to tell him until after he had died of a brain tumor), and replace Pete Best with Ringo Starr, who had a cooler name[3] and in an emergency could drum with his nose.

Back in Liverpool, the group was signed to appear at the Cavern Club, a dark, squalid dive patronized by dark, squalid divers, waterfront toughs, politicians disgraced in sex scandals and bored housewives from the suburbs, many hooked on gum, an addictive drug that caused the jaws to

2. A British slang term meaning "engigments."

3. They were unaware that he had changed it from Rheingold Starfarkuss.

The Amazing
Hair Trick

It was the Beatles who in 1963 began the world trend toward long hair. The truly incredible thing was that, at the time, the Beatles' hair was *short*. Just look at any contemporary photo of them if you don't believe it.

Why then, if the Beatles' hair was short, did the public think it long? The answer is simple: in 1963, everyone else's hair was very, *very* short.

clench and unclench incessantly. It was there that the Beatles would meet, fall in love with, and marry the man who would Change the Course of History.

Brian Epstein was the scion of a gay, middle-class, Jewish family that owned not only a large music store but also its own piano. Unknown to anyone, however, he also led a secret life as a respectable businessman. Out for a stroll in a pleasant fog one day and distracted by his usual fantasy of Clark Gable in chartreuse underpants, Epstein fell into a hole in the sidewalk and suddenly found himself in the Cavern Club, listening to the Beatles. Impressed by their verve, their insouciance, their *je ne sais quoi*, and their tight black jeans, he immediately stood up and offered to become the group's manager. A vote was held among those in the club and the motion passed 17 to 4, with only John, Paul, George, and Ringo opposed.

The new manager quickly took command, insisting on being addressed as "Field Marshal von Epstein, sir" and changing the Beatles' image by locking them in his bathroom until they agreed to bathe. While they were frolicking in the tub, he burned their smelly rocker rags and then presented them with stylish matching suits which he had commissioned from Carnaby Street's swingingest designer, Robert Hall. (Unfortunately they could not yet afford lapels.) At gunpoint, he forced the foursome to get shaggy haircuts with bangs, while also hiding their stash of Brylcreem.[4] "Now," he told them, "you are presentable and I can introduce you to me Mum. If she approves, I'll make you famous."

4. A well-known goo of the period, sometimes addictive.

Early in their career, the Beatles sometimes turned to petty crime to make ends meet. Here they race through an alley after robbing a pub.

True to his word, Epstein made them famous immediately, hiring a horde of teenage girls to chase the Beatles through the streets screaming and sobbing. When puzzled bypassers inquired, "I say, what's all that bother?", strategically stationed Epstein operatives would reply, "Why, them's the Beatles, the number-one pop group in the land, you iggerant, silly sod."[5]

Before you knew it, the group had a recording contract, major airplay, a dozen hits, and all the lapels they could eat. They became known as the Fab Four, after their favorite laundry product. Soon enough, hiring professional screamers became redundant, as they had been joined by amateurs, millions of them, all afflicted with a mysterious new ailment that became known as Beatlemania. A predecessor of mad cow disease, this plague was caused by kissing Beatle records; there was no known cure. The devastation it wreaked was catastrophic beyond measure; an entire generation screamed out its vocal cords and was left mute.

It was only natural that when the government organized the Brutish Invasion, so brilliantly described in the preceding chapter, the first band pushed out of the plane was the Beatles.

5. English slang for "schmuck."

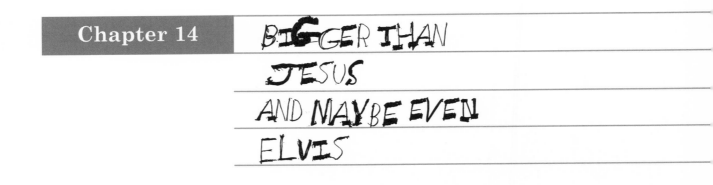

Chapter 14

BIGGER THAN JESUS AND MAYBE EVEN ELVIS

On February 9, 1964, the Beatles were introduced to the American public by Ed Sullivan—yes, the same Ed Sullivan who had given us Elvis a decade earlier. For most people that would have been enough, but not Sullivan. Oh, no, he had to be a big shot.

As the four hairy young men from Liverpool took the stage, some 73 million Americans watched their TV sets in utter astonishment, unable to believe what they were seeing—a man as dull and untalented as Ed Sullivan with his own show. They watched the Beatles too. The effect was magical. Lorinda Fressil, a teenager at the time who, against all odds, is still a teenager today, remembered what it was like in her recent autobiography, *Fressil on Fressil*:

> It was weird because when I watched them on TV that night, I was like, "Hey, what's the big deal?" But the next morning, I woke up and all I could think was, "The Beatles! I gotta have all their records! I want to be Paul's love slave! I want to march eastward under their banner and liberate the Holy Land from the infidel Turks." I still believe there was some kind of subliminal mass hypnosis thing going on that has never been revealed because, let's face it, *NSYNC is way cooler.

After appearing on the Sullivan show and dating Lorinda Fressil, the Beatles went on a concert tour of America, making them the first pop stars to play huge outdoor sports stadiums, not counting the Reverend Billy Graham. With Beatlemania at its height, the fans screamed so loudly and continuously

The Beatles leave the U.S. Capitol after telling Congress, "Remember, all we have to do is snap our fingers and all your daughters will follow us. So make sure our records are played constantly on every radio station."

they couldn't hear one word sung by the band whose music they loved above all else. But they didn't notice because, of course, they were very sick.

Returning to England in triumph (actually a whole fleet of Triumphs), the Beatles received many accolades and plaudits, most of which they sold to pawnshops, as they trusted only cash. The Vatican named a Pope after them, John Paul. The President of Mexico sent them a ton of his finest Acapulco Gold; the sultan of Oman, his youngest daughter.[1] U.S. President Richard Nixon put them on his Enemies List. Tiffany's created a new kind of jewelry that it named the ring, after Ringo. Even Queen Elizabeth honored the boys—though, being somewhat unclear about what they did, she designated them an artillery regiment in the British Army.

Refusing to rest on their laurels, which were too thorny for comfortable napping, the Beatles made their first movie, *The Knights' Hard Day*. The story of a four-man British band that achieves great popularity playing rock and roll, it was hailed by the critics as an immensely creative work of

1. After the Beatles tired of her, she briefly married Rod Stewart and eventually ended up as a TV weather forecaster in Wales.

imaginative fiction. But not all their actions met with approval. When John told a reporter that the Beatles "get more girls than Jesus," jealous televangelists around the world erupted in anger (wiping out several towns and villages) and burned their little black books in protest.

But the Beatles paid no attention; they were too busy growing, evolving, maturing as artists, and rutting like weasels. Announcing that they were giving up live concerts because too many people were attending them and ruining their privacy, the four retreated to their secret laboratory[2] and began a series of dangerous musical experiments that would Change the Course of History. Gone were the simple, joyous, upbeat jigs and polkas such as "Me Love You," "She Love He," "Me Love Do Love Me," and "Do Love Me, Me Lovely Love" that had propelled them to glory. Instead came increasingly complex harmonies, ambiguous lyrics, and postmodern semiotics anticipating the literary deconstruction of Barthes and Derrida and the cooking of Julia Child. The ground-breaking *Rubber Duck* and *Involver* albums, with hits like "Norwegians Would," "A Strawberry Feels Forever," and "Kill and Mutilate the Taxman," won the Beatles a well-deserved promotion from mere pop stars to artists. No longer were their albums found in record stores; now they were auctioned at Sotheby's or hung in the Louvre.

George Harrison patiently explains to Ed Sullivan that Ed should leave the stage because the Beatles are in the middle of a song.

2. In 1997, archeologists located its ruins beneath Margaret Thatcher and dug up several mummified groupies and the tomb of Brian Epstein, who's going to die in the next chapter. (Hope this doesn't ruin it for you.)

But it was their 1967 masterpiece, *Sgt. Pepper's Lonely Hearts Club Band*, the first album ever to sound almost like all the songs on it had something vaguely to do with each other, that at one stroke doubled the size of the universe and made it possible to finally end world hunger. Hailed as the first musical novel in operatic form, *Sgt. Pepper* served notice that the Beatles could transcend the heretofore limited rock-and-roll genre by playing their songs in nineteenth-century military uniforms with a symphony orchestra backing them up. Not only that but somehow or other they had mastered the extraordinary trick of making music that sounded exactly as if it had been played by people who had taken large amounts of hallucinatory drugs.[3]

From this incredible peak of fabulosity, there was little left for the Beatles to achieve and so, with their usual high spirits and protean creativity, they set about the difficult challenge of falling apart. It took several years to accomplish but the effort was certainly worthwhile. As top rock critic Gruel Mucus would observe:

> *So long as the Beatles were on the scene, other bands felt insecure and often cried. At night, they had nightmares of being smothered. They could not grow, they could not develop, they could not get enough groupies.*

So true, so true. And yet, at the same time, so sad.

---

3. The author has never taken hallucinatory drugs. I say if you must have hallucinations, why not obtain them honestly through good old-fashioned mental illness?

FABULOUS FACTOIDS
Better Than Best

Everyone over the age of 50 knows that original Beatles drummer Pete Best was replaced by Ringo and thus became the all-time preeminent symbol of just missing out on a great thing. But few people realize that Best himself had earlier replaced another drummer named Ted Fribble. Fribble had only been with the Beatles for a week when he got into a knife fight with George Harrison over a girl both lusted for and was voted out of the band. Today, he is a bitter, broken man who looks back on his days as a Beatle with undisguised loathing. "I hate them all," Fribble says, "and am sorry only fifty percent of 'em is dead. They ruined me life. I could've been the one replaced by Ringo and thus become the symbol of just missing out on a great thing. Instead I am forgotten and that usurper Pete Best gets interviewed all the time on all those whatever-happened-to bits on the telly. It ain't fair."

Chapter 15   MUSICAL MISERY TOUR

Brian Epstein did a silly thing one day. He dropped dead.

It was from natural causes.[1] Without Brian there to nag, the Beatles went to pot and sometimes LSD. They started dressing like hippies, sprouted facial hair, and contended that love would end the Cold War and cure cancer, often adding, just to drive home the point, "I am the eggman, I am the walrus, goo goo goo joob." Naturally, everyone under the age of 30 immediately did the same. Those over 30 grew frightened and clung tightly to each other, occasionally whimpering.

Even worse, the Beatles decided to manage their own business affairs, founding a corporation, which they cleverly called Apple Corps. Realizing the next day that corporations were boring and, furthermore, incomprehensible to artistic types like themselves, they left on a vacation to India, hoping that in between visiting tourist attractions they could study Oriental mysticism and learn to make Apple Corps vanish. It did, taking millions of Beatle dollars with it. Within months, it was Apple Corpse.

In India, the Beatles fell under the influence of the noted Hindu reform rabbi and talk-show guest, the Maharishi Mahashish Yogi Berra, who had attained the highest state of consciousness a mortal can achieve: being stoned without inhaling. (A feat never yet duplicated, except by Bill Clinton.) Though John, Paul, and Ringo were soon expelled from his holy presence after being caught trying to peek up a female disciple's sari during a levitation class (and then refusing to say they were sorry),

---

1. In other words, an overdose.

George remained behind to learn the sitar, which is much like the guitar, except that it is played in the seated position.

The next Beatles album, *Abby Rowed*, featured this much-quoted lyric:

> *Here comes the sun, cock-a-doodle.*
> *Here comes the sun, cock-a-doodle.*
> *Sun, sun, sun, here it comes*
> *through the bathroom window, LOOK OUT!*

This gave rise to a bizarre rumor that the Beatles had written the album on drugs. Not only that, fans somehow misinterpreted the cover photo of Paul lying in a coffin with his hands folded on his chest as a symbolic message from the band that he had died. Of course this was patently absurd—he was merely in a coma,[2] and quickly recovered—but the "Paul is dead" rumor developed a surprising life of its own and to this day is believed by everyone in Serbia as well as Oliver Stone.

By the time the *Whitish Album* (so called because some sort of unidentified powder seemed to be abundantly present during the recording sessions) was released in 1969, tensions in the band were so obvious they were even mentioned at the Vietnam peace talks in Paris.[3] The truth was that the Beatles were moving in different directions. Paul was becoming more and more interested in making solo albums for which he sang, played all the instruments, and

Permitted by treaty to enslave one female of their choice from any country they visited, the Beatles carry off pretty Belgian captive Annamarie Blechtag before departing Brussels in 1966.

2. Natural causes.
3. U.S. Secretary of State Henry Kissinger offered to bomb the Beatles' supply lines if it would help resolve matters but the British government declined his generous proposal.

packed his own lunch; George yearned to visit the Himalayas to record the legendary All-Yeti Zen Choir; Ringo wanted to go home and take a nap ...and John had met Yoko.

Yoko Ono was an artist who was so avant-garde she actually had an abstract body and existed only on an ethereal plane. It had recently landed in New York, disgorging her consciousness, which had been vacationing at higher elevations than most humans can bear. Her real name was Yoko Weinblatt but she acquired a new last name at art school where fellow students would scream "Oh, no!" whenever she raised her hand to speak in class. John met her at a sit-in[4] and was smitten or so it was written in Britain. (He was the most political Beatle except for Ringo, who had once attended a social-studies class in high school.)

As John would later explain to America's most respected TV journalist, Merv Griffin, "To me, Yoko represented what I had been looking for as long as I could remember: a woman." The couple immediately went to bed together, summoning the press pillowside to announce that they would remain in the missionary position as a protest until either the Vietnam War ended or John Wayne stopped making movies. It was a good concept but about two hours later John had to go to the bathroom so the protest fizzled as he pizzled.

As soon as Yoko learned that John was a Beatle and, worse, that there were three others, the group was doomed. She began attending the recording sessions for their new album, *Leave Us*

---

4. A type of social event common during the '60s. Similar to a kaffeeklatsch but resulting in an arrest record.

Be, and glared at Ringo until he became so nervous he began singing on key. Once he had fled the studio in tears, she trained her baleful gaze on Paul, who promptly handed her a press release announcing the breakup of the Beatles. He then walked outside and formed a new band with his wife, Linda, who promised to learn to play an instrument for the occasion.

One thing was now painfully obvious to everyone: George's infatuation with the sitar was getting really annoying. Also, the Beatles were dead.

Despite their deadness, the impact of their music on Western Civilization is incalculable, although a large accounting firm in Milwaukee has had three overweight CPAs named Marvin working on it since the early '80s.

The four members went their separate ways, pursuing their musical dreams and occasionally waking up to eat. For a time, rumors persisted that the Beatles would get back together for some special concert. Once, they met by sheer chance in a four-way car collision in Akron, Ohio, and harmonized on a few bars of "O Sole Mio," but that was as close as they ever came to a reunion.

In 1980, a "John Is Dead" rumor surfaced, owing to a false news report that probably began as a prank by the fun-loving Ringo. Despite its manifest implausibility, the rumor is still believed by millions of people today (though not by Oliver Stone or anyone in Serbia) and just goes to prove how gullible people can be in this age of instant but unreliable information.

John makes a charming and witty speech introducing Yoko to his fellow Beatles. Unfortunately, they have left the room, a harbinger of the acrimony to come.

Chapter 16

SPAWN OF BEELZEBUB

There were always those who felt that the Rolling Stones, not the Beatles or even Abba, were the world's greatest rock-and-roll band. Mick Jagger, for example.

But ultimately it was not simply a matter of musical taste; whether you preferred the Beatles or Stones said much about your personality and character. People who were happy, intelligent, well-adjusted, popular, clean, decent, and punctual tended to be Beatles fans. Those who were evil, cretinous, scabby, drug-ridden, filthy, criminal perverts liked the Stones.

As for your author, I personally take no side in the controversy, remaining strictly neutral.

But it must be admitted by any fair-minded person, as well as a few foul-minded persons, that much of the Rolling Stones' "bad boy" image was manufactured by a sensationalistic media. After all, despite a few arrests, riots, deaths, sexual debaucheries, and drug dependencies, no member of the group has ever been convicted of cannibalism or necrophilia.

It was 1961 when the nucleus of the band, Jagger, Keith Richards (who later shortened his name to Keith Richard to make signing checks easier), and Brian Jones, were first approached by the Prince of Darkness. Everyone, even the most talented among us, needs a big break, and this was theirs. At the time they were just typical British schoolboys—though perhaps not as handsome as most—unable to relate to anything in their barren environment except records by American rhythm-and-blues musicians and the naked photographs of the Queen Mother as a young flapper that were peddled on every street corner.

"Hiya, kiddos," said the Horned One after materializing before them as the three slept off a night of carousing in a public park one morning. "Wanna pull down 60 million quid per annum and have birds all over the world beggin' you to shag 'em?"[1]

Naturally, the boys quickly said yes, as anyone would, and Satan produced one of his standard contracts, to be signed as usual in the blood of a flaming virgin. "I remember him bein' particularly keen on us trouncin' the Beatles," Richards recalled in a 1992 interview on *The Barbara Walters Special*. "He kept repeatin', 'Those fuckin' goody-goodies. They're so fuckin' *cute.*'"

Handling the management duties personally, Mephistopheles told the boys to look scruffy and unkempt, grow their hair a full half inch longer than the Beatles', use four-letter words in public and show contempt for bourgeois values. Later, of course, this would all become de rigueur for rock stars but at the time it was daring and innovative.

"I was a bit dubious at first," Mick is quoted by historian Doris Kearns Goodwin in her book, *Roosevelt, Churchill, and Jagger*, "but he said all this nasty stuff would make the parents hate us and then the kids would love us. Turned out he really knew what he was doing. You had to respect that kind of professionalism."

Adding Bill Wyman and Charlie Watts to the lineup, the Stones started turning out hit records and then headed for America. When they put in their obligatory star-making appearance on *The Ed Sullivan Show*, the Archfiend provoked a riot in the audience. Teenage fans broke chairs, howled at the moon, and terrorized

Annoyed with fellow Stone Keith Richards for appearing onstage sober, Mick Jagger calls up the powers of darkness and turns him into a cake.

1. Source: *Encyclopædia Britannica.*

older audience members by giving them "noogies." Flustered, Sullivan announced, "Good Lord, what have I done? I never should have legitimized rock and roll. I should have known it would come to this. I see now that I have done a terrible, terrible wrong. I must repent!" He began tearing out his hair and beating his breast, then ran from the stage in obvious distress, entered a monastery, and was never heard from again.

As the band's fame increased, its members grew more independent and began resenting some of the demands made by their bilious manager. "He said me and Mick had to write our own songs," Keith Richards told a reporter for *Guns and Ammo* magazine in 1989. "Just because Lennon and McCartney were writing all those hits for the Beatles. I said, 'Christ, how are we supposed to write music? We're stoned all the time.' He says, 'Well, it doesn't have to be *good*. It's only rock and roll, for cryin' out loud. And never, *ever* call me Christ.'"

Nevertheless, the two did write, somehow turning out such rock classics as "Satisfaction," "Honky Tonk Women," "Let Me Bleed You," "(You're Just a Little Piece of Crap) Under My Thumb," "Let's Spend the Night Together but First Let's Have Sex," and "You Can't Always Get What You Want but I Can."

After Brian Jones died in 1969,[2] the band replaced him with Mick Taylor and went on another hugely successful American tour. By now, the conflict with Old Scratch had become even worse. "Mick was in tears," Lucifer told Mike Wallace on *60 Minutes* in 1987. "He said, 'I can't take any more. All those women, all those drugs, all that posing as a jaded, epicene cad, and these stupid fake lips I have to wear all the time, it's just not who I am. I need to find a nice girl, settle down, raise some kids, and join a church.' Frankly, his blubbering made me want to puke."

Finally, in 1969, the Stones worked up their courage and told the Beast they wanted out of their contract. "He just laughed in our face," Bill Wyman told the *Daily Forward* in a 1994 interview. "He said, 'What part of the word "eternity" don't you understand?' But when Mick told him we'd hired Johnny Cochran, F. Lee Bailey, and Alan Dershowitz to sue him, he suddenly went all ashy white."

El Diablo told the group he had decided to release them from their contractual obligations, but first they would have to do one more thing for him. Anxiously, the Stones agreed. The Rotten One said it

---

2. Natural causes.

would be a tribute to their fans, a free outdoor concert at a place in California called Altamont. "What a relief," said Mick, a broad smile breaking over his tense features. "We were afraid it would be something bad."

WHO'S THE BEST?

What Beatles Fans Say	What Stones Fans Say
☞ Lennon and McCartney wrote songs that will live forever.	☞ Keith looks like he already *has* lived forever.
☞ John was a witty, literate, multitalented genius.	☞ No Rolling Stone ever married Yoko Ono.
☞ Beatles sang, "Why Don't We Do It in the Road?"	☞ Stones *did* it in the road. Also on the sidewalk, the roof, the lawn, the woods, the parking lot.
☞ Six words: "Sgt. Pepper's Lonely Hearts Club Band."	☞ Six words: "Get out of my way, asshole."
☞ Ringo drummed like a man possessed.	☞ Mick dances like a demented gay gremlin.
☞ Paul could croon a sweet ballad or shout the blues.	☞ Mick could take on two groupies simultaneously while completely wasted on smack, coke, and Jack Daniels.
☞ Beatles kept evolving to new levels of creativity.	☞ Keith single-handedly disproved the evolutionary hypothesis of survival of the fittest.
☞ Beatles quit while they were ahead.	☞ Stones won't quit until they're rich enough to found their own country where all drugs are legal.

Chapter 17

BOB GETS HIS ROCK OFF

In July, 1965, the Newport Folk Festival was proceeding much as it had for over 340 years: with earnest men in work shirts and sincere women in work skirts singing heartfelt songs about oppressed coal miners in Kentucky, persecuted field hands in Mississippi, and blocked novelists in Paris, while plucking acoustic guitars before an audience in a state of elevated political consciousness, many of them requiring only one or two more credits to graduate to full sainthood.

Suddenly, a gaunt, pale figure with an unruly attitude and arrogant hair shambled onto the stage, followed by several musicians. Incredibly, they plugged their banjos and harmonicas into electrical sockets! And then they began playing what sounded suspiciously like…no…it couldn't be…but oh my God, it was…rock and roll!!

There was a moment of shocked silence. Then hooting and jeering broke out. Next came threats, screams, gasps, belches. People began throwing fruit, eggs, rotten yogurt, live grenades, mahogany credenzas from the Louis XV period, midgets, anything that came to hand. Men were fainting, women brawling, children spewing green bile and rotating their heads 360 degrees, dogs sniffing each other's hindquarters. In short, it was a scene of total, apocalyptic chaos unlike any that had been seen since the Hindenburg crashed into the stock market, unleashing the Johnstown Flood and sinking the Titanic.

Bob Dylan had gone electric and electricity would never be the same.

What had led folkdom's rising star to take this revolutionary step? Good question, because I just happen to have the entire case history right here in my hand:

He was born Robert Saccoandvanzetti Zimmerman in Tupelo Falls, Minnesota, on May 24, 1941, the son of Jewish parents who had been unjustly exiled from New York after being falsely accused of disliking lox.

Though bright, he became alienated at school because the other students thought of him as different. This may have been because he habitually wore a button that read, "I'm different." Upon graduation, he trekked to New York's Greenwich Village, where all vaguely artistic young people went whose vocational choice was "legend." Now he fit in perfectly because there everyone wore a button that read, "I'm different."

In the late '50s, there had been a folk-singing revival, spurred by the Kingston Trio's hit, "What Happened to Your Neck, Tom Dooley?" It told the tragic story of a poor boy who is bound to die and is advised, "hang down your head and cry," even though "get yourself a good lawyer" would appear to have been better counsel. Now, thousands of young people desiring to sing folk songs with an authentic Appalachian twang came to downtown Manhattan to learn how it was done. It was in this Creative Milieu, a singles bar where a lot of young people hung out, that the aforementioned youngster from Minnesota changed his name in honor of his idol, the great Marshall Matt Dillon of *Gunsmoke*. (Bob was never a good speller.) After learning that Dillon was merely a television actor and not a real lawman, he promoted his number-two idol, the great folk singer Woody Guthrie, to the top slot.

Woody Guthrie had come out of the Dust Bowl in the Depression and, after getting himself vacuumed, traveled the highways, byways, driveways, flyways, cryways, and Ididitmyways of America, making his living by entertaining hobos[1] on freight trains. As he did not realize hobos were penniless alcoholics, Guthrie remained poor and obscure. However, he had an enthusiastic cult following among the nation's idealistic youth, also known as Communists.

---

1. A primitive version of today's homeless person, though vastly more amusing.

Guthrie wrote many memorable songs, including the stirring "This Land Is Your Land." Let's all take a moment right now to sing it together. Okay, ready? A-one and a-two and ...

> *This land is your land*
> *This land is my land*
> *So how come you got Maui*
> *And I got Riker's Island?* [2]

Now just the women.

Seeking out his new top idol, Bob found him seriously ill-tempered in a Folksingers' Administration hospital in the Bronx. Though contemplating a coma and close to lunch, Woody retained his visionary vision, counseling the younger man, "I am your father, Luke. But if you oppose the Empire, I must destroy you." Confused and dejected by this puzzling advice, Dylan rode the subway back downtown and considered giving up folk singing, returning to Minnesota, and joining his father's used-pet rental business. Fortunately, he lacked the bus fare.

He began frequenting Greenwich Village's coffeehouses, [3] espresso bars, and barbershops. Catering to free-spirited bohemians, artists, writers, students, and existentialist philosophers— you know, bums—these establishments enthusiastically welcomed unknown young musicians, allowing them to play without charge. Eager to make his name, Dylan sang while accompanying himself on guitar, harmonica, accordion, and flugelhorn, often simultaneously.

Bob Dylan (seated, second from left) with the Hibbing High School Banjo Rascals as a teenager in Minnesota.

2. A bleak slab of landfill housing New York City's jails. Do I have to explain everything to you people?

3. Think Starbucks with beatniks, exposed bricks, and prices about 80 percent lower.

But unlike the other "folkies," who rendered traditional airs such as "The Blue-Tail Fly," "Greensleeves," and "Ninety-six Bottles of Beer on the Wall," Dylan performed his own original compositions. Because the audience paid no attention, preferring to discuss the rottenness of the corrupt establishment among themselves, Dylan was able to escape the harsh criticism, often delivered in the form of overripe fruit, that so often crushes an innovative artist before his sensitive genius can flower. On the downside, he never actually learned how to sing. But with his voice, it wouldn't have helped.

In any event, he developed into the hottest young folk-singing star in America (running an average temperature of 104.6 degrees) and thus was able to go to Newport and generate electricity. And without even noticing, he invented folk rock. The truth was that all along, Dylan had been leading a double life. While dressing, eating, and reproducing as a pure folkie, he'd been listening on the sly to rock and roll. And rock and roll taught him what folk singing desperately needed to become to compete in the modern age: a lot louder.

His brilliant insight would Change the Course of History.

Silent Bob Speaks!

In October, 2004, the sphinxlike Bob Dylan published a shocking autobiography. The book, Chillin' With Dylan, *dispelled many of the myths, fallacies, misperceptions, and psychotic fantasies that had clung to the iconic troubadour like barnacles to the side of a barn. Unfortunately, as is usually the case, the truth was infinitely less interesting. But here it is, anyway:*

Fallacious Myth	Tedious Reality
Bob authentically expressed the concerns of American Youth	Actually just expressing his yearning for a good pastrami sandwich
"Personal" songs were autobiographical	Songs were all based on one obscure novel by Balzac
Was hippest guy who ever lived	Idolized Wayne Newton
Made pilgrimage to Holy Land for spiritual quest that nourished his soul	Just trying to get away from nutty fans
Wrote "Blowin' in the Wind" to prick a nation's conscience	Lyrics came to him during acid trip
Spoke in riddles and ciphers that held profound meaning when deciphered	Habitually utilized pig Latin
One of the greatest philosophers and poets of his time	One of the greatest philosophers and poets of his time

Chapter 18

ZIMMERMANIA!

The '60s were a time of protest. There were civil-rights protests in the South, antiwar protests in the North, anti-East protests in the West, and protests everywhere against those who dared to protest. But it was Bob Dylan who got the idea to set these protests to music. Without him, there would have been no marches to sing at the marches and today we would be living in some endless morass of conflict, unfairness, and corruption instead of the beautiful world we now inhabit.

Dylan's early songs were filled with outrage against injustice, which, after solemnly considering both sides of the question, he decided to oppose. "Blowin' in the Wind," later adopted as a progressive anthem, was originally a fierce protest against littering. "The Times They Are A-Changin'" was a sarcastic comment against the stupidity of disrupting people's lives twice a year by switching from standard time to daylight savings and back, and "A Hard Rain's A-Gonna Fall" was a ferocious attack on the fools who refused to wear rubbers or galoshes on cloudy days.

Or so it seemed. But you could never really be sure because Dylan usually dealt in highly personal poetic imagery, obscure symbolism, and ancient curses from forgotten tongues to help conceal whatever point he was making. This was a clever ruse to make sure that his enemies wouldn't be able to understand his message and then feel the need to punch him in the face. Unfortunately, it also confused his friends. Thus, "I ain't gonna work on Maggie's farm no more" was taken by some as a *cri de coeur* against the exploitation of Mexican bean pickers, others as a call to drop out of society, and still others as a tirade aimed at a sexually demanding girl friend.

Many other singers recorded Dylan's songs of protest and were influenced by his style, though no one attempted to imitate his voice for fear of injuring themselves. The folk-singing group Peter, Paul, and Mary (whose real names were actually Abraham, Isaac, and Sarah, which their manager thought were too Jewish) had a number-one hit with "Blowin' in the Wind" and Sonny and Cher rose to fame with "I Got You Babe," Dylan's instructional ditty on how to shoot a an ex-lover turned stalker.

But Dylan also sang love songs that were surprisingly tender and romantic:

Over drinks, Bob Dylan explains to yet another crushed fan that he did nothing special and was never a prophet or the voice of his generation but is just an ordinary guy who happens to be amazingly wealthy.

Robert's Secret

When Bob Dylan agreed to do commercials for Victoria's Secret, it wasn't easy for the legendary troubadour to strike the right note. In fact, his first effort was rejected. It went like this:

Oh, what did you see,
my blue-eyed son?

Oh, what did you see,
my darling young one?

I saw string bikini panties with dead
fish all around them,

I saw a low-rise Brazilian tanga
on a hacked-up torso,

I saw an Asian detailed side-slit slip
with blood that kept drippin',

I saw a room full of sports bras
all covered with vomit,

I saw a white merry widow
all ripped and gone rotten,

I saw ten thousand V strings
whose strings were all broken,

I saw lace trim camis and bun pants
in the mouths of rabid hyenas,

And it's a hard, and it's a hard,
it's a hard, it's a hard,

It's a hard sell come this fall.

Continued on the following sidebar ☞

You taste just like a woman

(Yes you do)

And you pace just like a woman

(Back and forth, to and fro)

And you say grace just like a woman

(Let me eat already! I'm hungry now!)

But you dress just like Milton Berle1

Another of his sweet love songs was a plaintive cry of longing, though one in which Dylan evinced a troubling confusion in the area of biological reality:

Lay, lady, lay

Lay eggs upon my big brass bed

I put down some hay

So you won't mess up the spread

I'm tired of chickens, they're so dirty and mean

They make noise all through the night

You're better lookin' and you're pretty clean

C'mon and try it, just push with all your might.

To the displeasure of some of his fans, Dylan refused to stand still as an artist, hopping from one foot to the other while he sang. Even so, he denied being part of the "movement." After a near-fatal roller-skating crash in 1966, he went into Seclusion, a small town in upstate New York, where he recorded the album *Bootleg This*

---

1. A notorious cross-dresser of the period.

with the band known as the Band (formerly known as the Orchestra before losing its string section somewhere on the road) while wearing an oxygen mask. Strangely enough, this improved his voice. Never officially released, the album was sold through the black market, though whites could buy it, too, if they knew the secret password. ("Here's five bucks.") The album was passed from hand to hand, since there was only one copy.

Upon getting out of bed, Dylan announced he had entered his "mellow" phase, though what with his tendency to mumble, it's possible he may have actually said "mildewed." He went to Nashville and recorded an album of country music, with a backup group composed of sheep, then went to Italy and recorded an album of operatic arias, then became a born-again Christian and recorded an album of gospel, then converted to Buddhism and recorded an album with Thelonious Monk, then became an Orthodox Jew and ate a bowl of chopped liver with a side of pickled herring, then took up photography and made a photo album, then converted to Confucianism and recorded "Chopsticks," then espoused vegetarianism and recorded an album pleading for peas among nations, then became a fan of the television series *The Sopranos* and recorded an album entirely in falsetto. Finally he mysteriously vanished only to reappear a week later in almost the same spot but with a third eye and a confused tale of extradimensional travel.

Throughout these interesting metamorphoses, however, he always remained an enigma, a nonesuch, an onager, a rhombus, and a mahout. And chances are he always will, at least while he is still alive. After that, all bets are off.

> *But then Dylan, genius that he is, got his mojo working and came up with this brilliant lyric for the winter campaign:*
>
> How many bras must a girl try on
> Before you can call her well clad?
> Yes, 'n' how many panties must her fingers inspect
> Before she goes out with some lad?
> Perhaps she may choose her a sheer camisole
> Or a hot little thong that is plaid.
> Your undies, sweet girl, are blowin' in the breeze,
> Come buy our flannels or you're liable to freeze.

Chapter 19   SURFS 45 RIGHT

In 1513, the Pacific Ocean was discovered by the Spanish explorer Vasco Nuñez de Balboa[1] but "Rocky" Balboa, as he was called by his friends, never figured out that you could surf in it, so Spain lost its empire and became a third-rate power and had to make do with flamenco instead of rock and roll.

By 1960, that part of the Pacific touched by California was clogged with half-naked teenage boys balancing on floating polyurethane boards and shouting, "Hey, dude, surf's up!" while gorgeous, tanned girls in bikinis waved to them from dry land and offered to perform wanton acts of a sexual nature for the first boys to ride the huge and frightening Pacific waves ashore. Thousands drowned in the attempt.

All this became known as the California Lifestyle, a dream so enticing that soon everyone in America wanted to be part of it. (So did everyone in Mexico and by now most of them are in California.) Ah, California! It was a shining vision spread primarily by the songs of one bizarre musical group composed of relatives, friends, and their therapists, lawyers, and accountants, all known as the Beach Boys.

Why they chose this mysterious name no one has ever found out.

---

1. Actually, some Indians had discovered it long before Balboa but they forgot to contact *The Guinness Book of Records* so they got no credit.

Though an estimated 18,790 musicians passed through the band over the nearly 40 very long years of its existence, at the core of the Beach Boys was a mad genius named Brian Wilson, his brothers Carl and Dennis, and their cousin, Mike Love. Oh, and some guy named Mike Jardine. Also, one day, the mailman came by and he was inducted into the band too.

But the most important figure in the saga of the Beach Boys was the Wilsons' domineering father, Woodrow, because without his unusual child-rearing practices such as corporal punishment

The Beach Boys insisted on authenticity in their music. Here, they do research before writing their 1969 hit, "Joyride," which contained the famous lyric, "Saw the car, admired it, got my tools, hot-wired it."

The Beach Boys whoop in triumph
after finding five identical shirts
in the right sizes on sale
at a clothing store near home.
They enjoyed the simple pleasures.

administered by real corporals (there was an Army base across the street), television never would have had a dramatic enough storyline to be able to make the classic 2000 miniseries, *Beach Boys: Another Screwed-Up American Family*.

Having spent their youth in the desert town of Hawthorne, California, prosperous due to its rich deposits of sand, the Wilson boys dreamed of the far-off sea. They were influenced by rockers such as Chuck Berry but also by the lilting harmonies of such pop groups as the Four Freshmen, the Three Stooges, and the Mormon Tabernacle Choir. Listening to "Scrub Around the Tub" by Bill Haley and the Comets[2] over and over one day, Brian had a vision. "Hey, guys," he called excitedly to his brothers, who were outside beating up a passing Guy Lombardo fan. "Get this! We play rock and roll but instead of everyone just screaming whatever he wants, we have like actual tunes and we all sing the same lyrics!"

It was an insight so audacious it would Change the Course of History.

The boys set off on an epic trek 29 miles westward to the seaside city of San Surfino, where they began making surfing music and quickly gained a command of the sport's arcane patois such as "Mount your board, dude!" and "Barkeep, pour me a brewski!"

At first they were unsuccessful because their electric guitars kept short-circuiting. But then they realized that they could play better in a studio than in the ocean and things went much better.

---

2. Played under the titles of the 1955 Tarzan film *Blackboard Jungle*, it was the first rock song featured in a Hollywood movie, though the classic 1953 Soviet documentary *The Heavy Metal Group Potemkin* depicted the alleged invention of rock and roll by peasants at a Ukrainian farming collective in the '30s.

Their first songs, "Surfin' USA," "Surfin' Safari," "Keep Surfin'," "I'm Surfin' and You're Surfin'," "Hey, Now We're All Surfin'," and "I'm Feelin' Kind of Surfish Over You" were all number-one hits. "California Girls" was also a huge hit despite being banned on some eastern radio stations because it implied that girls residing in other states had smaller breasts.

The group considerably widened their range with their second album, *Enough Already With the Surfin'* (which in England was titled *A Certain Surfeit of Surfin'*). They had discovered an entirely new theme: cars. Songs such as "Surfin' in my Hot Rod," which told the story of a boy who dies when he drives his Corvette over a cliff into the ocean to try to drag-race on a wave, captured the imagination of America's teenagers and propelled the Beach Boys to new heights, eventually causing altitude sickness.

But Brian, his restless genius chafing against the limitations of hit singles, AM radio, and his tight jockey shorts, had become dissatisfied with the conventions of the rock-and-roll form. He retreated to his bathroom and spent the next twelve years working on a legendary breakthrough masterpiece album, aided by equally legendary amounts of LSD, which was in those days provided free of charge to rock stars by drugstores in order to liberate their minds from humdrum reality, unleash their imaginations, and let them feel totally uninhibited in case they wanted to remove their clothing and leap off the roof.

Rockin' Interviews

Brian Wilson

of the Beach Boys

Q. Are you happy?
A. No.

Unfortunately, by the time the perfectionist Brian finished the album, the Psychedelic Era was over, everybody was in clubs dancing to disco, his brothers had gone to barber school (eventually opening a hair salon called The Bleach Boys) and nobody wanted to hear the surfin' sound even if Brian was no longer making it. Brian put the only copy of the album into a dresser drawer and forgot about it. There the lost masterpiece languished for 35 years, during which time the dresser was donated to the Salvation Army and then bought and sold by various owners. In 2003, it was found in one of Saddam Hussein's less ornate palaces in Iraq by an American National Guardsman, who turned the album over to roving inspectors for the Rock and Roll Hall of Fame who had been searching for it for decades. The album, titled, *What's There to Smile About?* was finally released in 2004 to wows, huzzahs, and woohoos. A *Rolling Stone* reviewer gushed: "Brian—he was the tall, dark one, right? Is he still alive?"

As for Brian, after successfully completing light therapy that lasted a mere 27 years, he rejoined the group, which now called itself the Beach Boys Plus Crosby, Stills, Nash, and the Captain and Tennille with the Pips. They toured the world playing their great old hits such as "Good Libations" and "Damn You, Rhonda, Gimme Back the Remote," giving audiences a wonderful jolt of nostalgia and sending them out humming the Beach Boys' trademark close vocal harmonies on the bus all the way back to the assisted-living facility.

Chapter 20

OLD KING COLE WAS A MERRY
OLD SOUL BUT THAT DIDN'T
MAKE HIM THE KING OF SOUL
OR EVEN NAT KING COLE

One night, rhythm and blues had its way with gospel and nine months later, soul music was born.

Virtually all the great soul singers started in church. Hardly any started in the synagogue. There had always been lots of joyous music in the black churches because the congregants realized that only by singing loudly and insistently could they make the preacher shut up for a while.

It was just a matter of time before they would notice how easily hymns could be turned into hits. Whenever you heard a soul man sing "Baby, I love you," you could reasonably surmise it had originated as "Jesus, I love you." "Angels on High Praise Thy Glory" was converted to "Gloria, You're My Angel" and the lovely "Almighty Lord, I Am in Awe of Your Gracious Bounty," with just a few minor changes, became "Sex Machine."

At first, soul was appreciated only by black audiences. Whites, a little scared of all the unbridled passion in the music, hung back and awaited permission from their mommies. Some of the finest soul singers aged and died while waiting for mass acceptance. It wasn't until the Rolling Stones stepped forward and said, "Hey, this stuff's okay; let's, you know, borrow some of it," that whites flocked to the new sound, which by then was rather old. When Ike and Tina Turner opened for the Stones in 1969, they were both well into their eighties.

Of all the great soul singers, the one with the most nicknames by far was James Brown. He was known not only as Soul Brother Number One (Soul Brother Number Two has never been identified, though we do know for a certainty that it was not Strom Thurmond) but also the Godfather of Soul, the Filet of Soul, the Hardest Working Man in Show Business, Mr. Dynamite, Mr. Sex Machine, Mrs. Calabash, and That Screaming, Whirling Wacko in the Purple Cape.

Without a nickname, you could not be a soul singer. Aretha Franklin, for instance, was Lady Soul; Ray Charles was the Father of Soul; Otis Redding was King of Soul; Wilson Pickett was President and CEO of Soul; Sam and Dave were Managing Editor and Publisher of Soul, respectively; and Percy Sledge was Grand Vizier of the Soulic Empire. But back to James Brown.

Born in Augusta, Georgia, he was naturally musical and taught himself keyboards, drums, and bass while still in the womb. At an early age, he was born and immediately headed north, with a brief stop for jail (he served a three-year sentence for driving without a car) to rub off the natural polish that hampered his art. Great soul music was rough and lowdown; finesse could ruin a young talent faster than drugs, women, gambling or excessive sarcasm.

Arriving in Cincinnati, Brown formed a group he called the Famous Flames, though none of them wore drag, and recorded a demo for King Records, a leading company in the soul and R&B field. But due to a postal error, the demo arrived at the office of Don King and Brown was forced to waste six futile years trying to win the welterweight boxing championship.

Yet he overcame this obstacle too, formed the James Brown Revue, and developed the sensational stage act that made him a legendary soul legend. Utilizing 63 musicians, eight backup singers, a cape holder, and five picadors, he sang and danced up a storm that left him sweating and bleeding and the audience in shock. It was a kind of mass sexual experience.

Every show ended with the hit, "Please, Please, Please." The lyrics were deceptively simple but Brown's emotional rendering and his kinetic body language made them evocative, awakening complex shades of feeling:

Please.

Please, please, please!

[Leaps into the air]

PUH-LEEEEEEEZE!!!

[Returns to stage]

Whoa!

[Spins three times, does plié]

Please, please, please, please, please.

Uh…uh…uh!

Oh, baby, baby, baby PLEASE!

Please.

[Full split, then jumps back to his feet]

Whut I mean, I mean pleeeeeeze.

Please?

[Cartwheel]

Please!!!

Please!!!!!!

Please!!!!!!!!!!

AIIIIIIIEEEEEEEEEEEEEEEEEEEEEEEEE!!!!!!!!!

[Dives into crowd, extricates himself, races up and down
the aisles, climbs up the rear wall of the theater, and walks
upside down on the ceiling back to the stage]

And, by the way, did I mention please?

No?

His hand caught in the piano lid,
the beyond-legendary Ray Charles
screams like a trapped animal.
Tragically, audience members
thought it was just part of the act
and sang along.

James Brown stops a 1984 concert to announce, "Some no-good S.O.B. has stolen my shirt and nobody leaves this theater until I get it back."

Sorry, baby, sometimes I forget.

PLEASE!!!!!!!

Ohhhhhhhhh no!!!

[Has full-scale seizure, collapses, foaming at the mouth, stops breathing. Medical team rushes out to perform open-heart surgery. Priest administers last rites. Cape holder wraps Brown in cape. Coroner pronounces time of death. Embalmer begins working on corpse. Suddenly, Brown leaps to his feet, arms outstretched]

Pleeeeeeeeeeeeeeeeeeeeeeeeeeease!!!!

Oh, yeah!

[Pandemonium]

In 1967, Brown briefly tried to calm down. But he was too excitable and, while trying to sing a slow, quiet ballad, ruptured his thymus. Doctors advised him to jump up and down on a pogo stick while juggling fruit until he returned to his natural state of frenzy, after which he was fine.

If James Brown was Soul Brother Number One and the Godfather of Soul, then Aretha Franklin was without a doubt the sole Mother of God. Or something very similar. The daughter of a minister and a gospel singer, or possibly vice versa, she quickly came to the attention of people walking past the Detroit church where she was singing in the choir. They dialed 911-SOUL and major record company executives rushed to the scene, fighting like snarling dogs over who got to sign up the talented girl.

Columbia Records won and turned Aretha over to Mitch Miller, a record producer who also had a bizarre television show on which a platoon of men in cardigans stood at attention while singing corny tunes. It was inexplicably popular. Naturally, Miller decided that Aretha Franklin should make albums standing at attention in a cardigan while singing corny tunes.

Her career languished until the legendary Jerry Wexler of Atlantic Records kidnapped her, shooting his way into an extremely nonlegendary Columbia recording session (several cardigans were punctured) and carrying her off to the recording studio in Muscle Shoals, Alabama, where the legendary Robert E. Lee had once sung "Stagger Lee" after losing a bloody battle. Wexler, who had also guided the careers of the very great but unknown (except to each other) Harold Schenkler and Irene Grinspoon, allowed Aretha to sing the gospel/soul music that instantly made her a star. Her first album, *Aretha Without a Sweater*, contained the Otis Redding song, "Respect," with its famous lyric:

> *R-E-S-P-E-C-T*
>
> *That's the way it's spelled by me*
>
> *R-E-S-P-E-C-K*
>
> *That's how it's spelled by illiterate morons*

Aretha went on to become not just some mere legend, like so many iconic figures, but a myth, a fable, and, finally, an allegory.

Beneath the Music

Incapable

Though an archetypal rock wild man in performance, offstage James Brown was strict and meticulous, a no-nonsense taskmaster planning each show right down to the performers' underwear (backup singers had to wear white, Fruit-of-the-Loom boxer shorts one size too small) and fining musicians who missed a note or breathed without permission. One horn player was stripped on the spot, tied to the piano, and given fifty lashes with a drumstick after he lost control and winked at a pretty girl in the audience. Capist Gink Hargitay was severely chastised one night in Pittsburgh when he allowed the cape to touch the stage floor before it could be draped around Brown's shoulders. But all the attention to detail ultimately paid off when James Brown was named 1987's Obsessive-Compulsive of the Year by the American Association of Psychiatrists.

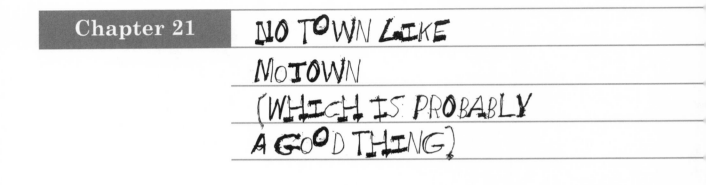

Chapter 21

NO TOWN LIKE MOTOWN (WHICH IS PROBABLY A GOOD THING)

While researching this book, I came across an astonishing fact, one which I daresay will rock you back on your heels, though why you're reading standing up I can't begin to guess: It turns out that Motown is not a real city but just a nickname for Detroit!

At any rate, the origins of the term appear to lie in the fact that Detroiters are ambitious people who always want mo', never less. This explains why American cars are so big. A typical driver of such large cars was the legendary Berry Gordy Jr., legendary founder of the legendary Motown Records.

Now I know you're expecting me to say that Berry Gordy was born in Tupelo, Michigan, and that his real name was Gordy Berry and that he changed it because he didn't want a free ride on the name of his legendary father, Chucky Berry, but I won't say that because, well, frankly, I am tired of lying to you and I can't do it anymore. I swear that henceforth I shall change my errant ways. From now on, I tell only the truth no matter how boring it is and may God strike me dead if I do not.

The third child of Ethiopian Emperor Haile Selassie and a giant carp that washed up on the shores of the Red Sea, Berry Gordy was born in Ulan Bator, Mongolia, in 1929.[1] Somehow he wended his way to Detroit (even though wending is illegal in most of the Midwest), proclaimed it his hometown, acquired a biographer, and went to work at the Ford auto factory as a wheel rounder. (Car wheels come into the factory square or rectangular and must be reshaped or they give a bumpy ride.) It was there

---

1. Ha ha! I'm an atheist! There is no God!

The Supremes show off some prize samples from their collection of skunk pelts, believed to be the largest in the world.

that Gordy discovered the principle that would revolutionize rock and roll: He would take the freedom and individuality with which blacks had invigorated popular music, put it on an assembly line, steam as much "soul" out of it as possible, and turn it into a standardized product. In this way, it could be marketed to millions of whites as "hot funky black voodoo music."

According to Motown myth, Gordy started in the music business as owner of a record shop that went bankrupt because customers wanted Fats Domino instead of the jazz Gordy favored. But like so many silly myths, this one is true. Borrowing $800 from a passing stranger, Gordy rented a cramped little one-family house at 2648 West Grand Boulevard and proceeded to turn it into the cramped little steel-and-glass skyscraper that became the headquarters of America's first black-owned music factory.

He called it Motown Records.[2]

Today that little skyscraper is a shrine visited yearly by millions of pilgrims who pray for sexual healing at the equestrian statue of Marvin Gaye in the atrium.

From the very start, or at least the middle, Gordy knew exactly what he wanted and how to get it. Speeding to the housing projects of Detroit in his big American car, he strode up and down the corridors, stopping at each apartment to listen for raw talent. Whenever he heard it, he would slide a contract under the door and move on to the next one. Soon the cramped little house at 2648 West Grand Boulevard that became a little skyscraper and today is a shrine was bursting with so much musical genius, a wall collapsed, and the Six Tops had to be renamed the Four Tops.

The Motown talent pool was immense, but sometimes it leaked and flooded the basement. Also, as I may have mentioned previously, it was raw. Berry Gordy knew that to become stars, his raw talent from the projects would have to be coached, shaped, molded, polished, and roasted, basting every two hours; then stir, allow to cool, and season to taste; serves twelve. So he hired a dancing coach, a make-up and hair coach, an elocution coach, a stage coach, a motor coach for when the stage coach broke down, and, just in case another studio challenged Motown to a softball game, a first-base coach.

"I remember it well," recalls Diana Ross, one of Gordy's early hires whose career, sadly, never went anywhere. "He dressed me in a top hat, white tie, and tails and made me say over and over again, 'The rain in Spain falls mainly on the plain.' Finally, I got so mad I threw my cane at him and shouted, 'Just you wait, Berry Gordy! Just you wait!' He threw his arms around me and kissed me passionately and we had a steamy love affair but then he walked out as I sang, 'Where Did Our Love Go?'"

Gordy established a family atmosphere at Motown, putting his singers on allowances and spanking them when they threw tantrums or wet their beds. "You have to be very strict with young artists and instill discipline," he often said. "Otherwise, they start to think they can make their own decisions and cross the street without supervision."

Utilizing the hit-prone songwriting trio of Brian and Eddie Holland and Lamont Dozier as well as talented house producers, arrangers, and musicians (especially the tobacco-addicted Smokey Robinson), Motown

---

2. Actually, he called it Tammie Records at first and then Tamla Records and, finally, Motown, but since reality is never as dramatically neat and satisfying as it should be, ignore that. Man, I am so sick of these annoying details that always screw up a good story.

developed its own distinctive sound. Some detractors called it a "formula," just because it always consisted of gospel-based pop emphasizing repetition, a strong beat and heavy backbeat, a change of key partway through the song, and the covalent bonding of elements to form a complex compound containing atoms sharing more than one pair of electrons. But that is unfair since all the Motown songs had *different lyrics*. Gordy preferred to think of his creation as "The Sound of Young America as Well as Certain English-Speaking Portions of Young Canada." He had the slogan printed on a big sign and mounted on the roof.

From 1963 to 1969, the Supremes, the Temptations, Smokey Robinson and the Miracles, Mary Welles, Marvin Gaye, the Four Tops, and the Five Bottoms recorded so many hit songs that finally they got bored because it was just too easy. And so in 1973, Gordy moved the whole Motown crew to Florida, where he built the nation's first black-owned retirement condo for aging rock-and-rollers. He called it SloMotown, and millions of fans have come to visit over the years. There they can see all their favorite aging stars and backup singers sitting around the pool, still compulsively bopping in unison with those trademark hand-and-foot moves that Motown's choreographers had designed for them back in the days when we were all young and vigorous and unafraid…not like now, when we live in fear, hiding in the gutters like rats, eating rotting scraps from garbage cans.

But make no mistake, we will fight our way back and defeat our nation's enemies nonetheless. And I don't care how long it takes. Ultimate victory will be ours!

GREAT
Rock-and-Roll Cities
DETROIT:
The River Town
That Got Big

It all began with the river. They called the river Detroit, a French word meaning "detour to someplace better." It was the river, a vital artery linking the Great Lakes with the Less Great Lakes that some 300 years ago brought the first settlers to the place they settled for. Many, many things occurred during those bustling three centuries that shaped a great city, far too many to be recounted in a tiny space like this. What could I have been thinking when I undertook such a hopeless task?

Chapter 22	THE HIPPIT

or

LORD OF THE MOOD RINGS

by Guest Author J.R.R. Tolkien[1]

Bilbo Baggins was tired. He had traveled a long way from his comfortable hole in the ground in Middle West and he had had many exciting adventures on the road. There were the chainsaw-wielding goblins who chased him through Texas, the hobbit-hating Highway Patrol officers who kicked him out of Arizona, and the wicked hooker who made off with the gold he won in Las Vegas.

Now Bilbo had arrived in San Francisco, a hilly town overlooking a magnificent bay full of wet, blue water. Bilbo was a hobbit. What is a hobbit? I am surprised you don't know. Haven't you read any of my books or seen the films? You should really get out more.

Today, by the way, there are no more hobbits; they were all wiped out (and in the most hideous way imaginable) by the ones they called the Mean Shits, which is to say, us. Oh, well. That's the price of progress.

Bilbo wandered about San Francisco taking in the sights until his hairy little feet hurt. All at once he realized that he had forgotten to bring his shoes. He had walked 8,537 miles and his hairy little feet were a horrid, bloody mess!

---

1 Okay, your hard-working author has written several spectacular chapters and now it's time for another break. This delightful piece was recently found among the papers of the very great and very dead Mr. J.R.R. Tolkien. Though I could not afford the price demanded by his greedy heirs, I was able to procure the gem nonetheless through a time-honored process known as grabbing it and running out of the building before they could catch me. Have a blast; see you back in Chapter 23.

Also he was hungry. He missed his snug little hobbit-hole back in Middle West with its larder that he always kept full of cookies and mouse-and-cheese sandwiches, heavy on the mayo. He was quite a fat hobbit, Bilbo was, and also one suffering from diabetes but he did not know it, since the hobbit medical establishment was, quite frankly, a disgrace. Pulling a handkerchief out of his vest pocket, he began to snuffle.

"Hey, man, what's bummin' you out?" said a voice behind him. "You on a bad trip?"

Bilbo turned round and saw what appeared to be a man with no face. But on second glance he realized there really was a face; it was just hiding beneath a huge mass of hair.

"O yes, I am on a very bad trip indeed," said Bilbo, in a polite tone of voice. He was hoping that the stranger was not a psychotic serial murderer who would slice his head off with a sword hidden beneath the hair. "And I wish I had never listened to the wizard Gandalf, who swore it would be

Peter Jackson, himself a hobbit, directs Sean Astin in the Golden Gate Park scene from the forthcoming epic, *The Hippit* (or *Lord of the Mood Rings)*, now being filmed in New Zealand.

good for me to 'get out and see the country.' But I assure you I am no bum. I am a very respectable hobbit with good references who happens to be a bit low on funds at the moment."

"That's cool, man," replied the hairy stranger. "You don't need bread here." He then cried out, "Hey, dig this groovy little cat with the furry feet."

A dozen hairy ones who had been loitering nearby shambled over. They were clad in rags of many colors and wore magical beads and shiny metal badges that proclaimed strange legends such as "Don't trust anyone over 30." This made Bilbo nervous, since he was 124.

"I'm Wavy Gravy," said the hairy man, "and we're from the Peace, Love, and Ketchup Commune. Peace, brother." He held up two fingers in a V.

"Pleased to meet you, Mr. Gravy, sir," said Bilbo. He made the V sign, too, assuming it was the way one said "hello" in this region. "I am Bilbo Baggins and I am on a journey of adventure."

"O wow, that is so far out," said a girl with a garland of daffodils in her long blond hair. Bilbo could only nod in agreement. Then he blushed when he noticed she wore no brassiere beneath her multi-hued T-shirt. Female hobbits always wore brassieres. They were somewhat prudish. Sometimes male hobbits wore them, too, but that is something I won't go into now.

"I'm Ruby Tuesday, Wavy's old lady," the blond girl said, proffering a lit cigarette loosely wrapped in brown paper. "Have a toke, Bill Bobaggins. This is, like, really dynamite grass."

These words were gibberish to Bilbo but he had not had a good smoke in quite some time. So he took a puff, even though the tobacco did not smell like tobacco. It was harsh and made him cough.

"Hey, man," said Wavy Gravy. "Why don't you jump in our game? Come on, we're truckin' over to the Haight."

Bilbo glanced about but did not see a truck. He was starting to feel a bit light-headed. "O dear," he said. "The hate? I don't know; that sounds rather scary. But thank you just the same, I'm sure."

But Ruby Tuesday seized Bilbo's arm and said, "Don't be uptight, man! Come to the Human Be-In with us!" Another girl, stout and frizzy-haired, exclaimed, "Right on!" and grabbed Bilbo's other arm. Together they lifted him right off the ground. And so, even though his plump little legs pedaled furiously in the opposite direction, Bilbo moved along with the throng of hairy people.

He did not know it yet but they were hippies. There are no hippies today, just as there are no hobbits. One day the hippies no longer seemed entertaining and everyone got bored with them so their contract was not renewed.

As his new companions bore him onward, Bilbo noticed that other hairy people were joining them. Soon there were hundreds. At last they all came to a big park filled with grass and flowers and more hippies. The hippies sat on the ground before a raised platform, passing those odd cigarettes back and forth until the air was filled with thick clouds of smoke.

"Boss vibes, huh, Bill?" said Wavy Gravy to Bilbo, who had been put down under a tree, where the members of Wavy's group had camped. "See, here in the Haight we're into our own scene, livin' in harmony with Mother Earth, free from the Man and his authoritarian, conformist oppression. Hey, you dig acid rock? 'Cause soon you're gonna hear some far-out cats jam."

"That will be very nice, I'm sure," said Bilbo. He had no idea what Wavy was talking about but he felt happier than he had ever felt before, though he wasn't sure why. "I would certainly like to

The Jefferson Airplane stands around doing nothing, a popular countercultural pastime in 1967.

have some jam, because I am very hungry, though I must say I have never had jam made of cats."

Indeed, Bilbo was so hungry the tree above him began to look like a huge celery stalk. It seemed odd to him that he had never thought much about celery before because now that he was giving it his whole-hearted attention, celery seemed one of the most fascinating subjects he had ever considered. He drooled.

"Got the munchies?" said Ruby Tuesday. "Here, try this." She gave Bilbo a brownie. It was the most delicious brownie he had ever tasted. He crammed the whole thing into his mouth and thought he must explode from sheer pleasure. With his plump cheeks bulging, Bilbo looked so comical that several hippies burst out laughing. And they looked so comical to Bilbo that he laughed, too. Soon all the hippies were rolling on the ground cackling and hooting. Several lost sphincter control and soiled their jeans. But that just made them laugh all the harder.

"O my heavens," said Bilbo, tears streaming down his cheeks and crumbs dribbling down his chin. "I haven't had so much fun since the time I was gang-tickled by three demented leprechauns who escaped from the hospital for the criminally fey."

Suddenly, the loudest noise he had ever heard blasted through the air. Bilbo was so startled he leaped up in a fright. "It's the Dead, man!" shouted Wavy in Bilbo's ear. "The Grateful Dead!"

Bilbo looked fearfully toward the platform up front. The people on it did not seem dead to him. They just looked like hippies playing guitars. But instead of plinking and plunking like normal guitars, these were howling and shrieking maniacally.

"Why are they grateful to be dead?" cried Bilbo. "I would be sad and a bit resentful. Are they dangerous? I ran into some dead people in Utah. They were zombies who chased me into New Mexico and they would have eaten me had Gandalf not appeared and changed them into beetle larvae with one of his magic spells."

Wavy did not hear him because the music was so loud and also because Wavy had his eyes closed and was waving his arms wildly about. Bilbo turned to Ruby and shouted, "Will they stop tuning up and start playing soon?" But Ruby must have misunderstood because she just passed him a sugar cube and said, "Time to drop some acid, man." Bilbo obediently dropped it. "No, man," said Ruby, picking it up. "Scarf it down." She popped the cube into Bilbo's mouth and he let it dissolve on his tongue. Nothing much happened for an hour or so, during which the Dead played the same song and the hippies danced, each seemingly lost in ecstasy. Finally, the Dead left and another group of hippies appeared.

"O wow," people shouted amid deafening cheers. "It's the Airplane!" Bilbo searched the sky but did not see any airplanes. He did, however, see a giant condor that snatched him up in its huge talons and flew him high into the heavens, where he was able to touch the sun before he turned into a large red rubber ball that came bouncing down to earth.

Back on the ground, though Bilbo would not have thought it possible, the Airplane was playing even louder than had the Dead. A pretty lady with long black hair was singing about a white rabbit. This story had been "borrowed" from a tired old tale called *Alice in Wonderland*, which is supposed to be a classic fantasy yet has no hobbits or dragons or swords or magic rings or heroic deaths. In my opinion it is vastly overrated.

After finishing it, the hippie princess sang another song:

> *When the truth is found to be lies*
>
> *And all the joy within you dies*
>
> *Don't you want somebody to love*
>
> *Don't you need somebody to love*
>
> *You better find somebody to love*
>
> *Maybe you could rent somebody to love*

When Bilbo heard these words, he realized with the shocking clarity of sudden enlightenment that he had no one to love. He was a 124-year-old hobbit with no job, no wife, and no little hoblets to inherit his hole in the ground. All the joy within Bilbo died and he burst into tears. Falling upon the ground, he began sobbing great, wracking sobs. Then his body broke up into millions of tiny, hairy molecules that rolled around getting lost in the grass which now grew as tall as a forest. A terrifying, roaring giant came along and deliberately stomped on the molecules, each of which screamed horribly as it was crushed into miserable atoms.

"Man," someone said. "You're having the worst trip I've ever seen."

"O me, O my," said Bilbo, slowly opening his eyes. "Where am I?"

"Why, you're perfectly safe in this lovely crash pad, Mr. Baggins," said a clean-shaven fellow with bright blue eyes who sat cross-legged before the mattress upon which Bilbo lay. The mattress was not on a bed but right on the floor. Bilbo gazed around and saw he was in a large room with no furniture and black walls full of posters with swirly designs. A dozen hippies were also in the room, sitting on the floor.

"Who are you?" said Bilbo.

"I'm Dr. Leary," said the white-haired man. "Tim Leary."

"Thank heavens I'm under the care of a doctor," said Bilbo. "I've had the most horrible nightmares of my life. I wished I would die."

"Well," said Dr. Leary. "You may view it as a negative experience if you choose. But I've taken LSD over 3,000 times and every single trip—even the ones when I descended into paranoid schizophrenic dementia—taught me valuable lessons about the nature of our society and my own internal geography."

"O man, that cat is so heavy," a hippie sitting in the corner said to no one in particular. "Can you dig it?"

"You see, my little friend," Dr. Leary continued, "the goal is to reach higher and higher levels of consciousness, until finally you bring about the unfolding of the fifth neurological-rapture circuit, freedom from static imprints, disciplined release of right-lobe ecstasy, and the joyful experience of Zen levity, which will liberate enlightened spirits to fully evolve, forming higher units in both neurological and physical Outer Space. Are you following me?"

"What—oh, yes," said Bilbo, who had begun to doze off. "Static electricity and nervous rapture. I dig it very much to be sure. You are a highly groovy man, man."

Dr. Leary spent several more hours imparting his philosophy to Bilbo, then slipped him an acid tab and said his good-byes. Later, a sleepy-looking hippie girl Bilbo had not formally met ambled over and asked if he wanted to ball. As Bilbo had always enjoyed playing ball, he said yes, and so the girl took off her clothes and fell onto the mattress beside him.

It was several months later that Gandalf appeared, without warning, in the hippie house. Bilbo, who had grown a beard and taken to wearing bell-bottom jeans and love beads, was in the kitchen, baking a favorite dish which he called Magic Mushroom Casserole. The ancient wizard seemed rather put out.

"Mr. Baggins," he said in a harsh tone. "What are you doing in this filthy hovel with these grotesque creatures? You are supposed to be wending your way toward the City of the Angels, where you were to have many adventures and finally slay the evil wizard called Manson."

"Hey, man," replied Bilbo. "Don't hassle me. I got a whole new bag now. Flower power is what's happenin', baby, dig?"

"What manner of preposterous drivel is this?" demanded Gandalf. "And where is the ring I gave you? Don't tell me you have lost the ring whose magic powers safeguard you from dragons, goblins, and unrehabilitated ex-convicts!"

"Fuck no, I didn't lose it," replied Bilbo. "I gave it to Sexy Sadie, my ex-old lady. Hey, did you know it changes colors according to your mood? Bitchin' bangle!"

"You are an imbecile," said Gandalf angrily. "I should have known better than to entrust so important a mission to a fool."

"You're really hung up on authority, you know that?" said Bilbo. "And you're into this whole outmoded good-versus-evil trip. Such a drag. You know what you need, Gandy? A chick. I bet you haven't been laid in about 300 years."

Gandalf looked as though he might erupt in a bitter outburst of reproach but he struggled to contain himself and finally just turned around and walked out of the kitchen.

"Yeah, later, man," said Bilbo, flipping the departing wizard the bird. Then he giggled, rolled his eyes, exclaimed, "What a fuckin' square," and went back to his cooking.

Chapter 23

EVERYBODY
MUST
GET
LOVED

In the late '60s, rock and roll got serious. Obviously, that places it outside the purview of this book, but being incorrigible, I will plod on anyway. So serious did rock and roll become that for a time it changed its name, insisting on being called simply rock. (Roll sounded frivolous, whereas rock was solid as a…well, it was quite solid.) Whether on or off a roll, rock had become one of the driving forces of the social and political upheaval known as the counterculture. It was now more than music; it was a way of life, though you still couldn't claim citizenship in it or even eat it.

What was the counterculture? Well, if you were young, had long hair, wore jeans, took drugs, had frequent sex with people not your spouse (or attempted to), wanted U.S. troops out of Vietnam (a tiny, insignificant country in Southeast Asia that had made the mistake of attracting the attention of the U.S. government) and had purchased a lava lamp (a lamp that operated by harnessing the power of any nearby volcano to light its bulbs), you were in the counterculture. Either that or you were an FBI agent assigned to penetrate it.

Because the older generation had sold out and was not cool and did not rock—and, on top of that, sucked—counterculture people did not trust anyone over 30. This presented a problem because almost everyone, despite all efforts to the contrary, eventually reached that age. Once they did, a terrible thing happened, even to counterculturalists: They immediately married, bought a house in the suburbs,

Best Defunct

Psychedelic Bands

of the Late '60s

The Electronic Overcoat

Named after a garment once owned by drummer Dirk Drummer, TEO, as its fans annoyingly referred to it, was notable for working a subtle drug reference into every song title. Among it biggest hits were "Mary Jane, I Love You," "Hey, Don't Snuff That Roach Yet," "I'm Dyin' for a Snort," and "Oh, God, I Think I've OD'd Again."

Existential Gumdrop

Perhaps the ultimate hippie band, this San Francisco group would hitchhike to out-of-town gigs and borrow instruments from locals. Gumdrop never had a hit record in its long one-year existence, but was legendary for its free-spirited concerts during which the band would "share its stash" with the entire audience. Gumdrop also pioneered the use of psychedelic light shows: the house lights would dim and band members would set their hair on fire.

Continued on the following sidebar ☛

voted Republican, discovered white wine, and thought about nothing but money. They were then called yuppies (an acronym for Young, Uncultured, Preposterously Proud, Irritating, Egregious Scum), and later, baby boomers (an acronym for Bad Apples Breaking Your Balls or…oh, never mind). These rules were very strict but had to be obeyed if you wanted to practice freedom and nonconformity, as all members of the counterculture did.

The guiding principle of the counterculture was love. As the Beatles put it in their succinct way, "All you need is love, all you need is love, all you need is love, love; love is all you need." The world's love supply was low, the counterculture felt—about ten billion quarts low—and needed to be drastically increased for any social or political progress to be made in the world.

By love, they meant: (1) frequent sex, and (2) not punching anyone in the face without a really good reason. Naturally, this impassioned espousal of love caused millions of people to hate the counterculture's guts. "Love is a subversive activity and could undermine our entire way of life," Vice President Spiro T. Agnew argued in a speech to his parole board.

Thousands of young people (and, yes, a few hobbits) converged on San Francisco to build an alternative society based on the aforementioned love plus sharing and community and a few other far-fetched notions now understood by science to be mere superstition. Can you imagine anyone today not believing in bourgeois materialism, for instance? The very idea is ridiculous.

Despite their determination to share, love, and cooperate, it was hard for the milling throngs of hippiedom to agree on anything because so many rock bands had formed in the San Francisco area that no one could hear anyone else speak. Among the best groups of the period were the Grateful Dead, Jefferson Airplane, Quicksilver Messenger Service, Big Brother and the Holding Company, United States Department of the Interior, Mountain of Chopped Liver, and Fluffo the Dog Who Walks Like a Man. Also, the Doors, the only band in Los Angeles (a cultural desert to the north), frequently visited, with lead singer Jim Morrison screaming, "We want the world and we want it now!" Frightened, the United Nations considered giving it to him but finally voted down the measure by a narrow margin.

A series of festivals and rock concerts held around San Francisco in 1965 and 1966 got the movement started and set into motion countercultural energies that would ripple throughout Western Civilization, almost tipping it over. (Then, as now, it was a lot shakier than it looked.) Hippies in exotic clothes—or none at all—danced, smoked marijuana, took LSD, and mingled with Beat Generation[1] icons such as poet Allen Ginsberg, writer Jack Kerouac, and bongo-playing radical existentialist Maynard G. Krebs. When word of all this fun filtered out to the country, middle-class college youth began flocking to San Francisco from all points of the compass as well as from cities and towns. By 1967, the population of the Haight-Ashbury district, San Francisco's hippie ghetto, was estimated at four billion people. There were hippie districts in New York and other cities, and hippie communes[2] in the hinterlands.

Holy Blue Menagerie

Starting as a Romanian folk group working the New England club circuit, Menagerie at first specialized in Appalachian hoedown jams mixed with Ethiopian *oud* music, but after sampling some hashish in 1966, switched to Canadian-style rock and roll. Essentially composed of one man, the versatile Eddie Jibbert, who played 17 different instruments, the band was cited by Kid Rock in 2001 as an important influence. (Jibbert died in an escalator crash in 1982 under suspicious circumstances.) Though never a headliner, Menagerie once opened for Moby Grape in Barstow, California.

The Codwallops

A family of musical hobos from Delaware, the Codwallops consisted of three children, two parents, an aunt, and a grandfather, lead vocalist Raymond "Buzz" Codwallop. Their hit single, "Peeing in the Snow and Elsewhere," charted at number three in 1967 but the group broke up the next year after conflicts over money and sex. Two-year-old Jimmy Codwallop later attempted a solo career but was laughed off the stage.

---

1. For an explanation of the Beat phenomenon, see the author's 1961 bestseller, *How to Tell If Your Neighbor Is a Secret Beatnik.*

2. Communes were similar to farms except you didn't have to get up early and work.

A counterculture artist paints a fellow hippie's face in 1967. Hippies were poor and could not afford canvas.

At this point the counterculture was over, as it had become the culture. From now on, all Americans would wear blue jeans, wear their hair long, listen to rock and roll, and take drugs. The counterculture had changed America forever.

Of course, the nonsense about sharing, community, and anti-materialism was quickly tossed in the garbage.

Chapter 24

THE DEADFUL GREATS

The importance of death to 1960s rock and roll can hardly be overemphasized, but I will try. In this most intense of all rock eras (and in case anyone ever asks you, the 1960s occurred between 1964 and 1975), dropping dead at an early age was considered a mark of greatness. Many musicians attempted it, but only the finest twelve or thirteen thousand succeeded.

One might well ask why. So might two or three, or even seven. And I will tell you why. *Because*, that's why. Because death was poetic, because it was dark, because it was, in the phrase of a later and even sillier generation, "edgy."

So many becauses, so few wherefores.

You see, in that primitive era, rockers were not as well educated as they are today. Most were college dropouts or, even if they were graduates, had majored in liberal arts and thus knew nothing. Many had been misinformed on the subject of death and didn't know it was permanent. By the time they found out, it was too late.

Yet if we look at the great sweep of history[1]—and who can ever resist doing that?—we can see that the dead-musician tradition began even before rock and roll was invented.[2] Wolfgang Amadeus

---

1. Which can be found under a rug in my living room.
2. By Thomas Edison in 1884, according to historians who discovered some important documents in a musty attic just in time to make it into this chapter.

The Dead, as people call the Grateful Dead now that most of them really are the Dead, had so many distinctions it's hard to know where to begin listing them: The ultimate psychedelic group. The ultimate jam band. The ultimate hippie band. The band with the most dedicated fans in rock and roll. The most boring band of all time.

So many questions are asked about this legendary band by children too young to know their story by heart as do all people over 45. For them, the children, our nation's future, here then are some authoritative answers given by the Dead's current manager, Toby Felthagensteinsonman.

Q. Why do their songs go on so long?

A. They never learned how to do endings.

Q. Did they really take immense quantities of drugs?

A. I wasn't with them then. I just came in recently.

Continued on the following sidebar ☛

Mozart started the custom, dying at age 35, which was the only thing that prevented him from becoming the immortal Wolfgang Amadeus Mozart. Next came Nathan Hale[3] and before you knew it, the whole thing was out of control, much like these damn footnotes. Stop it![4]

To better understand the phenomenon, we now zoom in on three of the greatest de facto defunct. Jim, Jimi, Janis...are you ready for your close-ups?

Jim Morrison

Jim Morrison was known as the Lizard King. This is because a tumultuous session of the World Reptile Convention voted him monarch for life. At least that's what he told his bandmates after a marathon acid trip. His group was named the Doors in the belief that their music would open the doors of perception and permit one to glimpse the hidden truths of the universe, such as that the universe is big and kind of gloomy. Their greatest hit was "Light My Fire," a passive love song in which the nearly catatonic singer begs his girlfriend to please do something, anything, that will get him interested in having sex with her. In his prime, Jim Morrison became a favorite of police officers everywhere. The men in blue would flock to his concerts, often becoming so enthusiastic they couldn't refrain from escorting him back to the police station and showing him their holding cells and handcuffs. In exchange Jim would exhibit his famed penis, which he liked to wave around in public whenever possible. Always open to avant-garde experimen-

---

3. Few people realize that had Nathan Hale not been hanged by the British after being caught spying, he undoubtedly would have gone on to be America's finest folk fifer.

4. Ha ha! Just try and make me.

tation, the Lizard King took up alcohol at a time when everyone else was still abusing drugs. After retiring to France following a long and full career, Jim died peacefully in his bathtub of a massive heart attack. Hey, it could happen to any 27-year-old. His tomb in Paris's Père Lachaise cemetery is regularly desecrated by legions of adoring fans.

Jimi Hendrix

Jimi Hendrix was the acrobat of the guitar. He could play it behind his back, blindfolded, and underwater. One time he played it with his testicles but admitted that was only to make Jim Morrison jealous. Considered by many to be the greatest rock guitarist of all time, and by others the greatest of some of the time, Jimi invented most of the techniques used by those who came after him, including picking, strumming, plucking, and generating weird electronic noises that make your hair stand on end. His too. Permanently. Born in Seattle, Hendrix emerged as a star while touring Europe with his group, the Jimi Hendrix Experience. This showed he was smarter than most rockers, who did not think of naming their bands after themselves and were thus condemned to remain unknown. One of his biggest hits, "Are You Experienced?," began as a want ad Hendrix placed in *Variety* to try to find a new drummer. His best known song, "The Star-Spangled Banner," became a classic and is still heard at sporting events to this day. Playing an electric, psychedelic form of the blues, Hendrix experimented with feedback, distortion, and barbiturates, the latter being his final experiment.

Q. Why did they go on, decade after decade, even though their act was stuck in the '60s?

A. You find a style that works, you stick with it.

Q. Is it true that Jerry Garcia designed a line of men's ties?

A. I think so.

Q. For someone who is unfamiliar with their music, which is the best Grateful Dead album to start with?

A. How the hell should I know? I just got here.

Janis Joplin put such raw emotion into her singing that she sometimes trembled and hyperventilated.

Performing in Florida in 1966, Jim Morrison and the Doors are pulled over and given a ticket for reckless drumming and singing while on speed.

Janis Joplin

Janis Joplin was an unhappy girl from Texas who proved that with nothing but talent, drive, and determination, you could transform yourself into an unhappy rock star. Singing the blues as only a black woman could, Janis, who was white, was so achingly vulnerable that little pieces of her heart were left strewn on stages across the nation, later to be snatched up by avid souvenir hunters and cardiac-transplant surgeons. Her super-intense singing was so nakedly revealing that she once said, "I make love to 25,000 people every night, and then go home alone." Selfishly, she never worried about the 25,000, who were off somewhere smoking a cigarette, wondering if Janis would ever call and hoping they hadn't picked up a sexually transmitted disease. Her myth began at the 1967 Monterey Pop Festival, where Janis wowed a crowd of festive pop drinkers. After that she was always called Myth Joplin. She scored a big hit with "Me and Bobby McGee," a song written by ex-lover Kris "Chris" Topherson, which contained the famous line, "Freedom's just another word for nothing left to lose," a direct steal from James Madison's "Federalist Paper No. 10." Tragically, when Janis was found dead in a hotel room from a heroin overdose in 1970, it came as little surprise to her fans because it was the third time she had been found dead in a hotel room.

Chapter 25

PARADISE
LOST

Woodstock. The name reverberates in the mind like some resonant gong struck by an oily stud in an old J. Arthur Rank film or the haunting cry of a million weary sea gulls circling the *Titanic's* watery grave.

Even those not born at the time of the greatest of all rock concerts or those who did not attend it but swear they did are stricken by the evocative power of the word.

Woodstock.

Say it fast and there's music playing; say it slow and it's almost like praying.

Instantly it transports us to another time, a time when love and peace ruled the planet, or pretended to, which is just as good. A time when the moon was in its seventh house and Jupiter aligned with Mars.

It was at Woodstock that the Age of Aquarius reached its zenith and the flower children reached puberty. It was at Woodstock that a nation found, lost, and misunderstood its innocence all at the same time.

---

1. Actually, it was a partly cloudy winter morning but the other thing sounds more poetic.

Beatific hippie girls frolic at the historic Woodstock concert.

I returned to Woodstock recently on a crisp autumn afternoon.[1]

On that hallowed site today, the forest has inexorably reclaimed what was once the famous cow pasture where the multitudes copulated so joyfully in the summer sun so many years ago. Now the vines and creepers have choked out the sweet clover and alfalfa; the PortoSans and Johnny-on-the-Spots where flower children took their comfort are rusted-out hulks; and hissing anacondas spit menacingly from the once welcoming shade trees.

Only the shattered memories remain. And the smell. Always the smell.

Such were my thoughts when, suddenly, my poignant reverie was interrupted as something snagged my foot, sending me sprawling headfirst into the fetid undergrowth. Regaining consciousness, I cleared away some rubble and uncovered the only remaining memorial to that long-gone moment in history. It was a simple stone monument in the shape of a nude, mud-spattered, tumescent hippie.

I could barely make out the once-shiny brass plaque on its plinth, so eroded was it by the fire and rain that periodically sweep these barren, wind-swept hills. It read:

Holy Shit!

That one magical phrase sent me hurtling through time. Suddenly, I was there. I had returned. I was, in a word, back. At a glance, I took it all in: the pert young breasts of ten thousand teenyboppers writhing in unison beneath their sweaty, tie-dyed T-shirts; the sweet, smoky fragrance of myriad joints blotting out the merciless July sun; the loudspeakers pleading for doctors to come to the emergency medical tent to stem the epidemic of overdoses; the hair, everywhere the hair; and above it all…the music.

The music!

Seventy hundred million supercharged amps of electric pandemonium coursing through the corpuscles and snapping the synapses of a generation.

Oh, yes, the gods rocked and rolled that holy day. The Grateful Dead, the Jefferson Airplane, and Santana were there as well as Crosby, Stills, Nash, and Young and…no, wait. I definitely remember Crosby and Stills but now I'm not sure about Nash and Young. Yeah, Young was there but he was solo. No, hold on, that was Van Morrison I was thinking of.

The Band, Bob Dylan's old backup group, takes a break at Woodstock.

Ziegfeld Follicles of 1968

Hair may not have been the first rock musical but it was certainly the hairiest. Written by Broadway legends Richard Rodgers and Oscar Hammerstein II, it told the story of Maria, a free-spirited nun who leaves the convent to take up with Curly, a charming hippie peace activist who makes a living selling drugs to stockbrokers while twirling a lasso. With such classic songs as "Oh, What a Beautiful Afro," "People Will Say We Need a Haircut," "I'm Gonna Wash That Man Right Out of My Hair," "The Furry Guy with the Fringe on Top," and a scene involving a fully clothed cast singing to a nude audience, *Hair* could not fail to be a smash hit. It ran for 1,716 performances, walked through another 433, and phoned in sixteen. Original leading man Sean Hannity went on to a successful career as a right-wing talk-show host.

Okay, I'll check on that but, no question, I definitely remember Jimi Hendrix, with his halo of frizz and his phallic guitar blasting notes that were simply impossible, especially after he set the guitar on fire. He tried to play "The Star-Spangled Banner" but too much of his ax had been burned away by then to produce anything but weird shrieks and wails.

One performer who still can't stop talking about his gig at Woodstock is folk-rocker Country Joe McDonald. "I had been the lead singer of Country Joe and the Fish, you know," he says. "But when I took the stage at Woodstock, I suddenly realized I was all alone up there. 'Where are the Fish?' I asked the crowd. 'Has anyone seen my goddamn Fish?' They just disappeared in that vast throng. Never heard from again. To this day, nobody knows what happened. But anyway, I found I didn't need any Fish. All I had to do was lead the crowd in an obscene chant against Johnson's war in Vietnam and they went crazy. So after that, it was just me, Country Joe, solo. Fuck the war, hold the Fish."

On and on the music went.

And still they came, the weary hippie hordes yearning to breathe free, avid to shed their encumbering jeans and T-shirts and frolic in the bosky dells, desperate to flee the highways backed up hundreds of miles, all roads leading that day to Woodstock, which of course wasn't really held at Woodstock at all, in case you're ever asked this on *Jeopardy!*, but at White Lake, near Bethel, so that Woodstock was in fact a misnomer, like Bunker Hill, or the New York Giants, who really play in New Jersey.

Finally, four hundred thousand strong, many sitting on top of others, fatally squashing them, the hippies reached utopia.

For the young and flowered, Woodstock was our Camelot, our Eden, our grand bouffe, our dinner with Andre, our bar mitzvah at Leonard's of Great Neck, our New Year's Eve and World's Fair and Last Supper all put together. And then, like all parties, the party was over.

Because scant days later came Altamont: our Gethsemane, our Armageddon, our Apocalypse, our Auschwitz, our Alamo, our Krakatoa, and our Enron, where a nation lost its innocence all over again[2] and a world turned grouchy and sulked.

At Altamont, a racetrack in California, all too far to the west of Woodstock, the stunned, not to mention stoned, multitudes watched the Rolling Stones watch the Hell's Angels stomp anyone who laughed at their tattoos. It was the most symbolic thing that ever happened anywhere, the name Altamont becoming synonymous with awfulness and signifying the end of the counterculture. Peace and love were officially retired, and strife and hatred put back in the number-one spot. The children had been deflowered.

But all was not lost. The movie made a fortune.

2. Leading journalists estimate that America's innocence has been lost well over twelve thousand times in the last fifty years alone.

Chapter 26

THE '70s: GATEWAY TO THE '80s

After the flower-powered utopian zeitgeist of the late '60s wilted and the hippies began mutating into yuppies, their hair getting shorter by the day, their jeans developing creases, their throats sprouting neckties, and their loins spewing Harvard-bound progeny, the authorities relaxed and declared the '60s over. "Whew," said President Richard M. Nixon in a nationwide address. "I guess there won't be a revolution after all and I'm safe at last. I just wish I knew what a zeitgeist was." However, it was now 1973, so the U.S. was plunged into a confusion from which it never recovered.

The seventies (nicknamed "the '70s" by some clever wag) would be an era in which rock and roll fragmented into a million different schools as well as reformatories and mental hospitals.

One of the divisions was hard (igneous) rock vs. soft (sedimental) rock. There had always been soft rock, of course, but now it grew positively gloppy as the former radicals, revolutionaries, Bolsheviks, and Wobblies turned inward. Not content with contemplating their navels, they also obtained X-rays of their livers and kidneys.

Typical of these old softies was James Taylor, whose lyrics such as "I've seen fire and I've seen rain, and I feel like flushing my head right down the drain" alerted medical science to the need for stronger antidepressants. As a result, Prozac would someday be born.

Taylor married another sadly sensitive singing songwriter, Carly Simon, disappointing Paul Simon, who had misplaced his Garfunkel and now was hoping to found an all-Simon musical dynasty. Instead, Paul got together with Taylor and Neil Young to form the gloom group the Downers. Their one album, *Get Down and Stay There*, caused millions of people to refuse to get out of bed, putting a crimp in the U.S. economy.

Young then became a partner in the firm of Crosby, Stills, Nash, and Young, specializing in close harmony, torts, and copyright law. He advised Joni Mitchell to record "Blue," which revealed that she was blue. Joan Baez, Judy Collins, and Carole King were all softly singing away, too, as well as Billy Joel, Elton John, Linda Ronstadt, Jackson Browne, and Jim Croce (who was more upbeat and cheerful, at least until he got killed in a plane crash). It was beginning to seem as though there would be no end to the sadly sensitive singing songwriter population explosion and the thoughtful people in the rock community were worried sick about how they could all be fed and housed.

But the hard rockers were also hard at work. Some of the '60s acts such as the Rolling Stones, the Who, and Pink Floyd were still going strong. British blues-rock bands like Cream and Fleetwood Mac swam into rock's mainstream, although how a rock could have a stream I have no idea. And the Hard Rock Cafe was founded so underemployed hard rockers could get something to eat.

Rick Nielsen, lead guitarist for Cheap Trick, is the only person in the world capable of playing this twelve-million-dollar custom-made guitar. With three or four more arms, he could play it well.

Aerosmith emerged as a leading group of the '70s. Its influence on rock and roll was perhaps best summed up by legendary dead rock critic Lester Bangs, who remarked that he had once had a picture of Aerosmith vocalist Steven Tyler on his wall for three months before realizing that it was neither Mick Jagger nor Carly Simon. The eternal mystery of Aerosmith, however, was how its members stayed alive decade after decade despite a level of drug use that would flatten a woolly mammoth. Medical science has requested Steven Tyler to donate his body for study as soon as he dies or, preferably, before.

But the true glory of the '70s was the explosion of new genres that proved once and for all that rock and roll was not some simple, short-lived fad but an enduring institution that would annoy us for the rest of our lives. (Actually, most of these new genres started in the '60s but I've spent enough time on the '60s and I have to move on.) The next seven chapters explore the most memorable of these new forms. Or is it the next eight? Okay, you just get started while I go and recount.

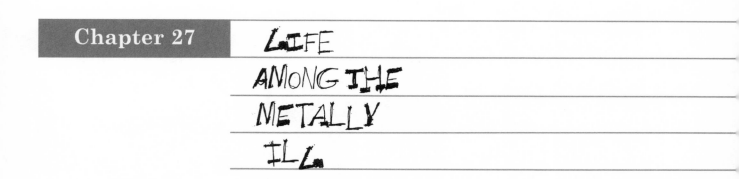

Chapter 27

LIFE AMONG THE METALLY ILL

Heavy metal had its origins in the late '60s when leading thinkers in the popular-music field began to realize that normal rock and roll was no longer loud enough.

The rapid growth of high-decibel rock concerts had caused partial or total hearing loss among millions of fans. Now they just sat in their seats blankly, not knowing when to hold up their cigarette lighters. This posed a threat to the vast music industry, which in that primitive era catered primarily to the ear.

Fortunately, American science was up to the challenge. In 1969, scientists at Conglomerated Techtronics & Sonics unveiled the Subatomic Particle Woofer, a device capable of amplifying music to an unheard-of, as well as unseen-of, seventeen million decibels.[1] This meant that people who were as deaf as an anvil with a broken hearing aid could again appreciate rock and roll, although they had to feel it through vibrations in the floor, some of which measured 4 on the Richter Scale.

The stage was now set for—heaven help us—yet another revolution. All that was needed was for the right group to come along to play unbelievably loud, distorted rock and roll which someone else could name "heavy metal."

It came in the shape of a blimp.

---

1. Tragically, hundreds of rhesus monkeys and white rats were lost in laboratory testing, mainly due to their heads exploding.

The members of Led Zeppelin stand in a field outside Barnstable, Massachusetts, in 1974, sadly watching a Ramada Inn burn down after they had accidentally set fire to their room.

Most musicologists and quite a few metallurgists agree that the greatest of all the heavy metal groups to plague society was Led Zeppelin. "Their metal is heavier than anyone else's," high-school science teacher Leonard Spivey often tells his senior honors class in physics, after demonstrating the principle with several dangerous and smelly experiments. "And so is their mettle."

Led Zeppelin was truly a groundbreaking group and when it wasn't breaking ground, it was usually breaking furniture. An entire book could be written on the art of hotel-room trashing[2] but it would have to devote several long chapters to Led Zeppelin. The Glenn Miller Orchestra did not trash hotel rooms. Neither did Ella Fitzgerald nor the Juilliard String Quartet. That is why they were not rockers. Led Zeppelin did and with precision and panache (a type of French pancake). Legendary drummer John Bonham never met a sofa he did not set afire and try to heave through a twelfth-story window (his legendary death in 1980 came when he forgot to let go of one) and equally legendary Robert Plant and Jimmy Page were once invited to lecture a night class at MIT on the most efficient way to tear plumbing fixtures from walls.

---

2. And if he can con some publisher into a big advance, you just know your author will write it.

Extraordinarily gifted, the Zeps did not orchestrate or rehearse their hotel-destruction epics but approached each in a spirit of inspired improvisation. Unfortunately, no trashing session was ever recorded or televised, so we can only rely on the word of other musicians invited to sit in or groupies invited to sit on, but most witnesses and insurance adjusters agree that the band's 1977 composition, Omaha Holiday Inn Suite 1237, was the finest thing of its kind ever done. It opened with Bonham riding a motorcycle through the rooms at high speed and climaxed with Plant and Page setting their manager's hair on fire, then spraying the flames with champagne. Still, it was Zep's 1979 decomposition, *Stairway to Hell*, that remains to this day the most requested bedtime story that Baby Boomers tell their grandchildren.

Almost as influenzal as Led Zeppelin (they once infected an entire continent in a matter of days) was another British heavy metal group called Black Sabbath. Led by the redoubtable, not to mention preposterous, Ozzy Osbourne, Sabbath dabbled in the occult, which would have been fine if they had just confined it to summoning up demons to kill and eat their enemies and kept it off the concert stage. Incorporating black magic into the act not only made Sabbath the first band with an occult cult following but also made possible the later careers of Alice Cooper, Marilyn Manson, and Shirley MacLaine.

A romantic, Osbourne sang of doom, carnage, plague, rapine, mayhem, and raving delirium, all of which he had personally experienced and enjoyed. Had he known he was fated to end his career as the bumbling, incomprehensible, drug-addled father in

Beneath the Music

Batman

Of all the many achievements in Ozzy Osbourne's remarkable career, probably the most memorable is the record he compiled in bat-head eating. Though not the first rocker to bite the head off a live rodent (Keith Moon of the Who did it in 1965, but not onstage), Ozzy was by far the best. He did it with a hair-curling demonic flourish and he did it more than 13,400 times, according to the PETA organization, which has vowed vengeance. "The bats always died instantly; there was no suffering," says Rod Clingworth, Osbourne's bat wrangler for nearly a decade. Where did they come from? "Oh, I know every cave in England," Clingworth chuckles. "I'd go down with a sack and catch thousands of the little fuckers, then keep 'em in a closet in my flat till needed." In 1984, Osbourne announced he had bitten his last bat head. Distressed fans bombarded him with letters of protest, but he remained true to his word, though occasionally devouring a live ferret.

an American TV sitcom, he undoubtedly would have tried out suicide as well.

At the time, however, though despised by all upstanding rock critics and most members of the PTA, Black Sabbath sold more albums than Cat Stevens and Rudy Vallee put together. Their first, *That Ol' Black Magic*, sold eleven jillion copies and their third, *Witchcraft*, sold sixty-two magillion. By the time the members of Black Sabbath had climbed into their coffins for a long-overdue rest, they had achieved such distinction that the Queen of England awarded them the honorary post of Lord High

Metallica's Lars Ulrich, Robert Trujillo, and James Hetfield inform Kirk Hammett that he has been expelled from the band for frequently appearing without sunglasses and also for looking happy.

Executioners of the Realm, according them and their descendants the right to put to death anyone they disliked.

In the dreary years ahead, heavy metal groups like Black Sabbath would sometimes be blamed for causing teenagers to commit suicide. This was patently unfair because studies reveal that many more people have been driven to take their own lives by the music of Yanni and John Tesh. Besides, as Ozzy Osbourne may have once said in a rare moment of lucidity, "It's a fookin' miracle that every fookin' teenager doesn't fookin' commit fookin' suicide."

Though England is where heavy metal began, if only in the sense of commencing, it was inevitable that America would produce its own version. After all, the U.S. had far more lunatics per square mile. Sure enough, American metal groups soon began springing up, often bowling over unwary people not agile enough to leap aside when holes in the earth opened beneath them.[3] Such bands as AC/DC, Metallica, Guns N' Roses, and others too numerous to exterminate spread across the nation uncontested. With their thumping, sluggish, distorted, repetitive, murky riffs causing a vast upsurge in over-the-counter headache remedies, many a pharmaceutical-industry fortune was made.

In the decades to come, heavy metal would grow so loud that neighboring countries would begin to complain. At one point, Mexico called the police, who came and issued the U.S. a stern warning.

But ultimately nothing worked. Even a nuclear strike failed. Metal could not be destroyed by any known means. There was no other choice but to ignore it and move on to the next chapter.

The Girls
on the Bus

Groupies had existed for centuries but had no name that could be printed in a family publication (not that this is one) until the late '60s, when rock bands became known as rock "groups." (Had this name change not occurred, women donating their bodies to needy rock stars would have been called "bandies" or possibly "band-aids") The women's and gay liberation movements of the '70s raised the status of groupies, who demanded and got better working conditions and drugs. At that time, female rock stars also gained the right to have groupies of their own. Today, the popularity and stature of a rock group or rock star may be determined simply by counting the number of groupies in or near the dressing room following a concert. Proud, dedicated, and highly skilled, groupies are working hard to make the world a better place for all of us.

---

3. These mysterious rips in the fabric of the time-space continuum may have had something to do with abuse of the environment, experts say.

Chapter 28

BAROQUE

AND

ROLL

To rock-and-roll purists, art rock (also known as classical rock, fancy-schmancy rock, and rococo 'n' rololo) was an oxymoron. Not only that, it was a hydrocretin and a polyimbecile. Rock and roll was supposed to be short, simple, trashy, and stupid so that it could appeal to teenagers. Art rock was long, complex, intelligent, and high-minded, so that it could appeal to pretentious teenagers.

For those in the hard-core rock establishment, the scandal was that art rock aspired, rather than perspired.

"The fools," cried Walter Trittick, recording secretary of the Hard-Core Rock Establishment, when informed that art rock was in existence. "This affected conceit must be suppressed before it corrupts the old and middle-aged. Ban it, I say! No, wait; that would be censorship. Murder it in its crib!"[1]

Oh, the exquisite irony of it all. See, rock and roll was originally a rebellion and now art rock was in rebellion against the rebellion. The former rebels had become the establishment and were down on the new rebels. Get it? See the irony there, huh? Huh?[2]

Anyway, art rock is thought to have originated in Florence, Italy, where Mickey Caravaggio, Mike Angelo, and Slam Raphael, three young artisans who had been sniffing paint thinner, founded Procol

1. Walter tended to get a bit overwrought and in 1978 was impeached after sneaking into Barry Manilow's hotel room and short-sheeting his bed.
2. Be patient. Not all the readers are as smart as you. Some need special attention.

Harum and recorded the gigantic hit "A Whiter Shade of Pale." It was this lovely song that started the whole tradition of art-rock lyrics consisting of completely meaningless gibberish. To this very day there are still people asking the question, "Who were those sixteen vestal virgins and why did they leave for the coast?" No one has ever found out.

The frilly genre then jumped to England, apparently spread by bacilli harbored by fleas carried by rats. There it exploded and shot off in a million different directions, becoming so dynamic and varied that it promptly died out. But while it lasted, art rock had a tremendous influence on astrophysics and Eastern European politics. Even now it is still secretly practiced by members of occult societies in the Gobi desert who live in yurts and form bands, playing nothing but wind chimes and the horns of musk oxen.

Here are capsule descriptions of a few of the artiest rockers in the art-rock pantheon, which is appropriate since many of them habitually (or in some cases, barbiturately) swallowed capsules:

The **Moody Blues** started in 1965 as a group of moody Englishmen who played blues. In 1967 they saved up enough money to buy a Mellotron, a new electronic musical instrument invented by Australian boomerang magnate Mel Lotron, which had the ability to imitate other musical instruments. Thus armed, the Moodies switched to art rock and amazed critics and fans with their uncanny ability to impersonate the Academy of St. Martin-in-the-Fields Chamber Orchestra under the direction of Sir Neville

A man named Art throws a rock. This should not be confused with art rock.

Rink Cycle

Many art-rock groups turned classical music to rock purposes; many wrote and performed rock operas. But only one band is known to have combined rock and roll, opera, and ice skating. In 1979, the Welsh group Celts in Kilts released its third album, *Götterdämmerung It All* and embarked on a world tour featuring an elaborate Wagnerian stage show on ice. Band members Rick Bleak (lead guitar), Ioffud Gryffter-Jones (drums), and Lunch Warren (bassoon/ synthesizer) all mastered the difficult feat of playing rock and roll while skating. Unfortunately, the tour was plagued by technical problems. (Warren's skates twice cut the amplifier cables and Gryffter-Jones had to have six different drum kits on the ice so he could play while accomplishing such maneuvers as a triple lutz.) Still, Celts in Kilts fans flocked to the show and showered the group with bouquets and teddy bears despite the protestations of critics such as Dave Mush, who called it "probably the most nauseating and egregious piece of tripe in the entire history of rock and roll."

Marriner. Their best-known song, "Knights in White Satin," recounted the tale of a band of medieval warriors with peculiar taste in combat gear. Other compositions were even less accessible. The Moodies, as their fans—and their psychoanalyst—called them, were so boldly original that their 1970 hit "Higher and Higher" actually had nothing to do with drugs.

Technically, **The Who** shouldn't really be classified as art rockers but they made the fatal mistake of inventing rock opera— and if that's not art rock, what is?—so I'm sticking them in this chapter. It has to be filled with something, after all, and would you rather read hundreds of words about Yes, Deep Purple, the Electric Light Orchestra, King Crimson, and Emerson, Lake, and Palmer? No. Not if I know you as well as I think I do. So... .

A merger of two early English groups, the What and the Huh, the Who was part of the first wave of British rockers that washed over America's shores, badly eroding them, and even then were considered by many experts to be superior to Herman's Hermits. Everyone, even Charles de Gaulle, acknowledged Pete Townshend to be the best leaping, windmilling guitar smasher of his g-g-generation, vocalist Roger Daltrey to be the best microphone twirler ever (they still had cords then), and drummer Keith Moon to be certifiably insane. Even though Townshend failed to achieve his famous ambition—"Hope I die before I get old"—he inspired many other rockers to do so. Keith Moon, for example.

When Townshend wrote and the Who recorded *Tommy*, the musical saga of a deaf, dumb, and blind pinball wizard who falls in love with the beautiful gypsy girl Esmerelda and is beheaded by the Pharaoh for his impudence, only to rise again as a phantom one-armed billiards champion, critics around the world sat up and took notice. Then they went back to sleep. Performed at Milan's venerable La Scala, *Tommy* caused a scandal when Italian opera buffs rioted because the lead tenor was not fat enough. In 1975, Busby Berkeley directed the commercial movie version. It starred a miscast Omar Sharif as Tommy but when he sang the poignant ballad, "See Me, Feel Me, Touch Me…No, Not There, You Pervert," audiences were greatly moved, usually right out of the theater.

Frank Zappa was sort of a cross between Charles Ives and Spike Jones. One of the thinnest men of his time, he wore a mustache and eyebrows so heavy and black they appeared to be painted on, in the grand tradition of Groucho Marx. Quick with a lethal scowl, he would not suffer a fool, though on occasion he would fool a sufferer. With more than sixty albums under his belt, causing an unsightly bulge, Zappa was a virtual virtuoso as well as a virtuous versifier who often induced vertigo in virgins. Leading his band, the Mothers of Invention, with the first electric baton, he played everything from jazz to classical, from rock to roll, from Amarillo, Texas, to Barnstead, New Hampshire. Testifying before Congress against censorship in 1983, Zappa aroused controversy when he said that [**CENSORED BY U.S. GOVERNMENT**]

Chapter 29

GLIT, GLITTER, GLITTEST

David Bowie was just another androgynous British rocker
with the looks of a Calvin Klein model until he dyed his hair orange, put on a shiny, otherworldly costume with huge shoulder pads and began calling himself Ziggy Stardust, rocker from outer space. This made him a star. All his competitors were wearing jeans and T-shirts, so Bowie was like, wow.[1]

At the time, jeans and T-shirts were considered "real." You were supposed to wear the same clothes onstage as off-; otherwise you were no better than some disgusting old show-biz phony in a tuxedo like Sammy Davis Jr. or Arturo Toscanini. But once David Bowie started dressing up in glittery costumes, it was okay for everyone in rock. (Actually, Bowie stole the concept from Liberace, another disgusting old show-biz phony, but you have to get your ideas someplace.)

Bowie changed his identity several more times, disguising himself as Zizzi Zazou, can-can dancer from Montmartre, and Myron Shmendrick, Jewish tailor from Delancey Street. The albums put out under these hip aliases sold millions of copies and, to this day, no one can remember a single song from them. Bowie went on to announce that he was gay and then married the beautiful Somalian model, Iman, confusing the public no end. Iman, too. (Sometimes she would ask, "Iman or you man?") Finally he went into movie acting, but either Rock Hudson or Doris Day kept getting the roles he wanted and his career waned.

---

1. Don't look at me that way. My publisher says I have to go for the youth demographic.

David Bowie denies he is a space alien at a 1976 press conference he called to dispel ugly rumors circulating in the supermarket tabloids.

Yet his influence was great. In the early '70s, Bowie traveled hither and thither (but, for some reason, never yon), a kind of Johnny Candyappleseed, strewing glitz and glam in his wake.

Mott the Hoople, an unsuccessful heavy-metal band, was contemplating a fatal heroin overdose in London when Bowie suddenly appeared before them in full regalia.

"Dare to be glam, lads," he commanded. "Dare to sparkle."

Stunned into obedience by the sheer force of his rock-star charisma, they put on nine-inch platform heels and mascara, allowed glitter to be sprinkled on their heads, and recorded a Bowie song, "All the Young Dudes." Within seconds, the song hit the charts and the charts were too intimidated to hit back. It won the band a huge gay following.

"Please," the Hooples begged Bowie. "Don't tell them we're straight."

Not to worry. Bowie was already off, sensing there was much interesting mischief to be done in the New World. All over America, there were failing rockers who just needed a touch of that special Bowie magic to set them on the right course.

Terry Blinfeck,

"DR. GLITTER"

Glitter, the branch of rock emphasizing androgyny, philology, weirdly shaped guitars, high-heeled boots, and lots of makeup, would not have been possible without the imagination of one man, Terry Blinfeck. For it was he who invented the sparkling glitter dust that gave the genre its name and its cheap, tawdry flashiness. Sprinkled on hair, clothing, skin, and food, glitter made rock stars twinkle as brightly as the very stars in the heavens, although viewing the former through a powerful telescope could be more than a little frightening. Born in St. Paul, Minnesota, in 1943, Blinfeck migrated to Minneapolis and studied chemistry, becoming a leading freelance scientist. Trying to invent an improved form of nerve gas in his home laboratory in 1965, he noticed that, following an explosion, the ruins of his split-level house now emitted an unearthly glow. From there to David Bowie…well, it was merely a matter of time. Today, owing to a series of lawsuits and prison terms, Terry Blinfeck is a forgotten man, lonely, poor, miserable, and living in his rusty, battered pickup truck, But none of that matters for he is a legendary giant of rock and roll.

Ignatz Paderewski,[2] an escaped mental patient who tuned lawn mowers for a living, was persuaded by Bowie to change his name to Iggy Stooge and become America's first punk rocker. Misunderstanding Bowie's instructions, Paderewski changed his name to Iggy Punk and became a stooge, founding stooge rock with his hit, "Curly Don't Love You No Mo', Moe." Iggy was the first rocker to smear his naked torso with peanut butter onstage, slash himself with sharp objects, and then dive into the crowd, which respectfully parted to allow him to alight unhindered. He was never injured, though, as he usually managed to land on his head.

Bowie also influenced Lou Reed and the New York Dolls to glam it up and as a result, they became seminal performers of the era though, frankly, I'm reluctant to discuss bodily fluids. Soon, thousands of America's most promising young rockers were bleaching their hair and trying on platform boots. The cosmetics industry and the heel industry became ecstatic as excited rockers realized you could go platinum by going platinum.

Then came Kiss. Founded by Gene Simmons, a New York public school teacher (and what that says about the New York public school system is another topic best left unexplored) with the world's longest tongue,[3] Kiss became a hit after its members donned bizarre costumes and began setting off smoke bombs, flares, and concussion grenades onstage, literally stunning their audience.

Kiss became known as "the band without a face," because no one had ever seen its members without their grotesque facial makeup.

---

2. Not the famed Polish pianist, just someone who happened to have the same name. Yet another odd coincidence in a turbulent saga filled with them.

3. On several occasions, the tongue escaped and rampaged through the city, terrorizing innocent citizens. Hundreds of people were licked senseless before it was shot with tranquilizer darts and returned to its proper mouth.

However, a major scandal erupted in 1978 when ace investigative reporter Bob Woodward revealed that all along they hadn't really been wearing makeup; they just had grotesque faces.

While critics were almost unanimous in reviling the group's thumpety-thump heavy-metal sound (which resembled a sledgehammer repeatedly striking a robot in the groin), the fans adored it. Thad Grepple, president of Kiss Ass, the band's fan club, explained the appeal to a crash-test dummy sitting in for an ailing Mike Wallace on *60 Minutes*, saying, "As fans, it is our job—nay, our *calling*—to fall blindly in love with mindless, irredeemable music."

And so it was that glam rock, also known as glitter rock, theater rock, freak-show rock, and dressing-up-like-mommy rock, became an established genre. As *Time* magazine observed, "In just a few years, rock and roll has gone from revolution to decadence, which is good because here at *Time* we're pretty decadent ourselves. Somebody want to pass the absinthe?"

Kiss in concert, 1975.

Chapter 30

DISTINGUISHED
PUNKS
OF THE
MODERN ERA

History tells us (if we're dumb enough to listen) that punk is an older phenomenon than is commonly believed. The first punks were a barbarian tribe that swept out of the Asian steppes sometime between 127 B.C. and 1422 A.D., wreaking havoc and dirty words upon all in their path. Mounted on swift, sinewy ponies, the merciless punk hordes provoked terror with their ratty clothing, surly attitudes, and the iron pins they jabbed through their own noses. Many villagers fainted at the sight.

In approximately 99 A.D., a punk army under Thregmar the Slovenly sacked Rome. Fortunately, by then Rome had already been sacked by the Huns, the Vandals, the Visigoths, the Ostrogoths, and the Minnesota Vikings, so there were no sacks left. The punk chronicler Osiric the Unconvincing called the meager pillaging, plundering, looting, and polluting there "the biggest waste of time I've ever seen; these guys are just going through the motions." Bitterly disappointed, the punks retreated beyond the Ganges and founded Punkistan, which survived till the sixteenth century, when it was converted to a flea market.

In the late nineteenth century, a wave of immigration washed a host of punks to America's and England's shores. Some stayed on the shore, much taken with tanning and kicking down sand castles built by toddlers. The rest moved on to the coastal cities, settling in the worst slums. (They weren't poor; they just felt more at home there.) Quickly assimilating, these punk immigrants enjoyed such

Joey, the tallest, strongest, and least photogenic of the Ramones, always stood in front, daring anyone to try and push him aside. His bandmates feared him.

cultural riches offered by their new lands as the Monkees and the New Christie Minstrels.

But the children of these immigrants were dissatisfied. These young punks and punkettes viewed the rock establishment as complacent, corpulent, and flatulent. Unbelievably, it now contained many musicians who actually knew how to play their instruments.

The shame! The betrayal! Even those rockers who were revolting against the rock establishment were revolting much too gently. The young punks realized that to revolt properly, you had to be *completely* revolting.

And they were.

Modern punk began in New York City in the late '60s where protopunkular bands like the New York Dolls, the Velvet Underground, and the Not Yet Punk but Close began playing in low-paying venues such as sewer pipes and crosstown buses. Then at a club in the Bowery called CBGB (an abbreviation of "country, bluegrass, and blues," none of which were ever played there), true punk emerged, slinking out of a dark corner behind the men's room. The movement was led by four brothers who were not related to one another called the Ramones. Dressed in black leather jackets to symbolize their reverence for rock tradition and torn blue jeans to cover their pale, flaccid buttocks, the Ramones took rock music back to its roots and then beyond, to its seeds. Their idea was to play louder, faster, and simpler than was humanly possible. They came poignantly close to succeeding.

The average Ramones song lasted eight and half seconds, though some were much shorter. For instance, here are the complete lyrics to their best-known song, "Glue Sniffin'":

I sniff glue

So do you

Woo woo woo.

The Ramones never had a hit record and for most of their career had to subsist on a diet of grubs and roots. They came to a

The Rules

of Punk

- ☞ Keep it short.
- ☞ Keep it simple.
- ☞ Keep it loud.
- ☞ No solos.
- ☞ No whining.
- ☞ Look skanky.
- ☞ Stay thin. There are no fat punks.

sad end when Johnny Ramone stole Joey Ramone's girlfriend, Ramona, causing the two bandmates to stop speaking, which made Dee Dee Ramone's voice wear out. Still, the group inspired more parents to commit suicide than any other band in history, certainly no small achievement. What's more, they inspired the greatest punk band of all time, the Sex Pistols.

Yes they did. Of course, it must be conceded that the Sex Pistols[1] started out with huge, unfair advantages in the punk world. The lead singer, Johnny Rotten (real name: John D. Rottenfeller), couldn't sing and the lead guitarist, Sid Vicious (real name: Sidney Viciousnogoodbastard), couldn't play guitar. Also, due to their elite punk heritage, both had great natural snarl with a high level of curse control and perfect vomit.

"When I first smelled these two, I knew they were gonna be the worst thing since Hitler," exulted Malcolm McLaren, the visionary rock entrepreneur and used-underwear-shop owner who created the Sex Pistols. Attracting considerable attention with their first (and also their last) album, "Never Mind the Bullocks, Get Me Some Oxen," the band exploited discontent with the British Royal Family with urbane and witty sendups such as "God Eat the Queen":

I dislike the Queen intensely

Yes, the Queen

That's who I mean

She's mean mean mean

The Queen Queen Queen

Sad and Nasty

The 1986 film *Sid and Nancy* told the world the greatest punk love story of all, a story so poignant and heartbreaking and repellent that it is said to have inspired Courtney Love (who appeared in the movie) and Kurt Cobain (who didn't) to fashion their own tragic romantic punk saga a decade later. Sid Vicious was, above all else, a man in love, even though it was heroin he was in love with. The debonair Sid spent two thirds of his day completely unconscious and the rest as a swaying, drooling, slack-jawed zombie who would walk into walls unless led in the right direction. But to American groupie Nancy Spungen, he was Romeo, Prince Charming, and Charles Manson combined. Together, the two lived out an enchanting, fairy-tale romance reminiscent of an African nature documentary about demented baboons in a death struggle with rabid hyenas over the rotting carcass of a diseased warthog.

---

1. Apparently the name was a subtle reference to some kind of genitalia.

For a time, the Sex Pistols showed great tenacity; Sid Vicious stayed with their tour of the Canary Islands even after dying from a heroin underdose. But tired of propping up his deceased partner, Johnny Rotten finally grew disillusioned, changed his name to Peter Putrid, and denounced his former group as "a bunch of hype," saying that "the Sex Pistols were never what we claimed to be, although frankly, I have taken so many drugs, I can't quite recall what that was."

Though punk could have honorably skulked into a back alley somewhere and died at this point, it adamantly refused, continuing to grow and fester. Wherever there lived young people enraged at the inequities and stupidities of a cold, uncaring world, the two basic options offering relief were inflicting mass casualties upon one's high-school peers or forming a punk group. Indeed, many punk aggregations have come and gone since the heyday of the Ramones and Sex Pistols, including at least one legitimate super-group, the Clash, whose story I shall fail to relate in a subsequent chapter. Enough is enough.

Chapter 31

THE NIGHT THEY DROVE OLD DISCO DOWN

WARNING

Never say the word "disco" in front of a rock-and-roll purist. He will kill you, without the slightest hesitation or regret, and then quietly go back to whatever he was doing.

Disco was music for people who were too shallow to be punks. Though it had no soul,[1] it did have a beat and you could dance to it. In fact, dancing was about all you could do to it. Listening was out of the question. Disco music was so vapid that it couldn't help but become a national craze.

The name was a shortened form of "discontinued," since no one expected it to last very long.

Disco began, as almost everything does, in the gay and black ghettos of American cities. According to psychology majors at a large, mediocre Midwestern university, it was adopted by people who were sick of the egomaniacal preening of rock idols and wanted to be egomaniacal preening idols themselves. They fervently believed that if they wore flashy clothes, took massive quantities of drugs, and danced under flashing strobe lights near a second-rate celebrity, they could fool themselves into thinking they were glamorous stars.

---

1. All the soul had been used up by soul singers.

They were aided in this creative hallucination by the great artistic breakthrough of the disco industry: eliminating musicians. Once those show-offs with their egotistical guitars and fascistic drums had been replaced by an anonymous DJ spinning records, the ordinary chump had more room to "do his thing," in the witty parlance of the day. Even better, the club owner got more profit.

After disco was declared an official fad in 1974 by an act of Congress, disco clubs appeared in all U.S. cities, towns, highway median strips, and military bases at home and abroad. President Gerald Ford took private disco lessons and reportedly once danced to a song by KC and the Sunshine Band with Indian Prime Minister Indira Gandhi in the Lincoln Bedroom. Whether coitus ensued is unknown.

Of all the disco clubs, the most famous was New York's Studio 54. Built in a remodeled football stadium, this tightly guarded, exclusive room allowed in only 54,000 carefully chosen individuals every night (hence its name). The official drug of Studio 54 was cocaine, selected by a vote of the patrons. On arrival, each received a complimentary packet of the stuff. You had to bring your own gold or silver spoon, however.[2] In case a customer's nose fell off from cocaine overuse, he was given a new one free by management, because grotesque disfigurement would have adversely affected the club's chic ambiance.

Eventually, the disco's owners were sent to jail after a jury convicted them of aggravated obnoxiousness. But before that sad day, it was generally agreed that Studio 54 was the world's greatest party

In the climactic disco scene from *Saturday Night Fever,* John Travolta strikes his iconic pose and shouts, "Oh my God! I'm having a vision that I won't make another decent movie for fifteen years!"

2. Of course the wealthier patrons had been born with one in their mouths.

since the legendary bash in Moscow at which Catherine the Great announced her engagement to a horse. Every night, glittering celebrities, cerebral glitterati, gibbering paparazzi, and slithering gibbons crowded in until their lungs imploded, dancing genital to genital and tongue to tongue, while outside, sneering bouncers jabbed pitchforks into wretched nonentities clamoring hopelessly for admission.

Studio 54 attracted a wild mix of show-biz personalities, railroad tycoons, diplomats, and hermaphrodites from many walks of life as well as several trots and gallops. Among its better-known habitués were Liza Minnelli, Henry Kissinger, the Duke and Duchess of Windsor, Wile E. Coyote, Lizzie Borden, Antonin Scalia, Madame Pompadour, Honus Wagner, Laverne and Shirley, and Keats and Shelley.

Discomania reached a peak with the release of the movie *Saturday Night Fever*. Starring John Travolta and several people who were never heard from again, the film was adapted from a fairy tale by the Brothers Grimm (who also sang the best-selling soundtrack for the movie, calling themselves the Bee Gees, in a falsetto so high that dogs all over the world howled for years afterward). It tells the story of a poor but hard-dancing ethnic youth from Brooklyn who is unfairly considered a cretinous lout by his insensitive parents and employers just because he is staggeringly stupid. At the local disco, however, he is worshipped as a god because of his whimsical feet and tight pants. When he breaks a leg while executing a difficult maneuver called the Donna Somersault,

How Disco

Did It

Dancing, medical researchers have recently discovered, is an essentially physical activity, utilizing a little understood process called "movement." Interestingly, disco music seems to "connect" in some mysterious way with our body's internal rhythms. The basic disco tempo is exactly double that of the human pulse rate while the typical timbre of string or choral harmonies uncannily mirrors the pattern of synaptical response in the human neural system. What this means in lay terms is that when disco music enters your brain, your feet go nuts and fling you across the floor of the disco until you are gyrating insanely with some six-foot-nine, whacked-out drag queen from Calgary. Once the process has begun, there is nothing you can do to stop it.

he is spurned by his snooty but redundant dance partner as "an ungainly, maladroit klutz" and commits suicide by eating sixteen pizzas with everything at one sitting. The entire city mourns and Rudolf Nureyev and Dame Margot Fonteyn dance naked at the funeral while the Bee Gees sing the haunting refrain:

Ah ah ah ah

Staying alive

OK, not really.

This ending was so depressing that the entire worldwide disco craze vanished during the final credits.

Revelers dancing
the night away
at Studio 54.

Chapter 32 — ALL THAT JAZZ ROCK

A typical fan
of Blood, Sweat & Tears.

Jazz rock was a hugely important development, despite the fact that there were only three jazz-rock bands in the entire history of jazz and also, by a strange coincidence, in the history of rock. They were:

1. **Chicago**
2. **Blood, Sweat & Tears.**
3. **I forget the third.**

Why were there so few jazz-rock groups? Because playing jazz rock was *really hard*. You had to learn not just one but *two* separate musical forms. These were, in alphabetical order:

1. **Jazz**
2. **Rock**

Most critics agree that a large share of the blame for creating jazz rock must be heaped upon the shoulders of Miles Davis. This is easy to do because, despite his being one of the greatest jazz trumpeters of all time, nobody liked Miles or his shoulders. Miles was so irritable that he would usually play with his back to the audience, which was his way of expressing to them the musical idea, "Oh, are *you* still here?" Being a certified genius, Miles did not have to bother being nice.

But with his historic (though not legendary) 1969 album *Bitches Brew*, Miles Davis achieved a synthesis of jazz, rock, and alliteration that sold 400,000 copies and won him a whole new audience composed of beer-drinking bitches. Though at the time some observers felt that *Bitches Brew* was the first jazz-rock album, a blue-ribbon panel of experts later established that what Miles was playing was actually rock jazz. However, it did usher in a new trend of fusion (not to be confused with the old trend of confusion).

Now getting back to Chicago and Blood, Sweat & Tears and whoever the third jazz-rock band was—come on, let's face it: they were rock groups that occasionally sounded a little jazzy. This was mainly because they had horns. Not in the sense of ibexes or impalas, you understand, but in the sense of trumpets and trombones. The horns afforded a distinctive sound since most rock groups had no horns. Why? Well, their members just plain didn't have the brass. Chicago and Blood, Sweat & Tears did. And that other group, whoever they were. And thus did they prosper and were fertile and their crops were abundant and their tribe increased.

Blood, Sweat & Tears was formed in New York in 1968 by veteran musician Al Kooper, but Kooper quit in 1969 for a solo career as a juggler, taking Sweat with him and leaving only Blood & Tears. Singer David Clayton-Thomas then joined the group, recording the hits "Spinning Wheel," "And When I Die," and "You've Made Me So Very Happy" (the lyrics of the last two being adapted from the will of John D. Rockefeller and the reactions to it of his heirs). Then Clayton left, taking Thomas with him but leaving David, and the group became Blood, Dave & Tears. It still played jazz rock, but without sweat it became too laid back and eventually stumbled, fell down, and hurt itself.

Chicago formed in 1967, naming itself after a large Midwestern city that the band's lead guitarist had always dreamed of visiting one day. Though he never actually got there, in 1979 the group added the words "University of" to its title and became accredited as a college, which it remains to this day, occasionally betraying its musical roots with a lonely trumpet heard wailing the blues from a funky chemistry lab late on some dark lonely night.

Chapter 33

HIX PICK SLICK LIX IN STIX

Since rock overwhelmed and absorbed all other types of music in the '70s, it was inevitable that sooner or later it would move to the country.

Of all people, it was Bob Dylan who first got on the hay wagon. Traveling in disguise to avoid wrathful urban rock fans, he slipped quietly into Nashville, which is known as the capital of country music even though it is actually a city. On arrival he headed straight for the recording studio, where he rounded up a bunch of Nashville cats, then found some musicians and began recording his first country album, "A Hard Rain's A-Gonna Fall and My Overalls Will Get Soggy Again," without even bothering to write any songs for it. That's how good Dylan was.

The album contained such immortal hits as "Why Did the Chicken Cross Highway 61?," "Like a Stolen Roan," "Hey, Mr. Tangerine Man," and "The Maggie's Farm Revisited and This Time I'm Not Talkin' Metaphorically Blues." But some critics felt that his duet with Dolly Parton, "Old MacDonald Had a Fern," missed the mark.

At any rate, when the album came out, numerous other rockers headed for Tennessee, which most had never heard of previously, and arranged throat surgery to enhance their twangs. As for the locals, they thought a rocker was a kind of chair and were too polite to correct anyone who believed otherwise.

Of the many country-rock bands that emerged at this time, one of the most successful was the Eagles, although after recording their big hit, "Don't You Leave Those Lyin' Eyes Lyin' Around Where Somebody Might Lie Down on Them, Lila," they switched to city rock and, finally, suburban rock.

Moocow, a band that pioneered country-girl rock, plays to a packed house in an Alabama nightclub.

Another was Dylan's old backup group, the Band, a group of Canadians living in upstate New York who dressed as off-duty Confederate soldiers and sang poignant rock ballads of the rural life among Arkansas poultry.

Of course, there were also those rockers who all along had been hiding out in the hills, brewing up white lightnin', and dueling the wild packs of idiot children who infested the backwoods, where they waited for gullible strangers who they could challenge to banjo duels. Johnny Cash, that old rockabillygoat, had returned to his southern roots, which he pickled and saved in jars for the lean winter months, and in the process became a country-music legend.[1] In an epochal moment in musical history, the actor/songwriter/ movie star Kris (Chris) Topherson landed in Cash's legendary backyard one day in a helicopter[2] to deliver a song he had written,

1. Which wasn't hard to do. There are millions of them.
2. Yes, it was a Cash landing; now let me get back to my narrative, damn it.

declaring, "Johnny, at last I have found you, you reclusive old son of a gun." To which Johnny replied, in his inimitable rumbling bass, "I'm in the phone book, you dimwit, and you have ruint the damn rutabagas."

Down in the bayou crouched Creedence Clearwater Revival, soaked up to their waists, sometimes singing of crawfish and sometimes sounding like a radical protest band. Then there was Willie Nelson, that old redneck hippie outlaw crooner from Texas. Was Willie rock and roll? Not really. Was he country? Sort of. Was he disco? No way. What was he then? How should I know? You think it's easy to figure out these weird, mixed-up genres? Come on. You had all these confused people. Like John Denver, a folkie, with a touch of country and a smattering of rock. You had Linda Ronstadt, who did country rock until she got tired of it and then sang ballads in Spanish. You had progressive country and soft country rock such as Glen Campbell and Kenny Rogers and you had the raw, cowflop-flavored sentimentality of country punk.

The truth, the terrible truth, if you must know it, is that rock and roll is pretty simple and after a couple of decades of it, most of the available patterns had been used up, which is why there was all this thrashing about looking for new categories to combine it with. A rock shortage was threatening the planet. Everything had been done. The apocalypse was near. I don't know if I can go on.

And yet I must, for if not me, who?

Worst

Country-Rock Song

of All Time

No contest! It was the Baptist Catfish Society's 1973 ditty, "Critters I Seen" (written by lead singer Sonny Bob Burpkin), which began with these immortal lines:

I heard a herd of aardvarks barkin' in the park

Then I seen them nekkid, stark

Just parked there in the dark.

Chapter 34

GUM TOGETHER RIGHT NOW OVER ME

Bubblegum has never gotten its due. Instead it has gotten doo-doo. Rock critics forever point out that most of the bubblegum bands didn't actually exist and call the style "childish, puerile, juvenile, infantile, immature, redundant trash."

Well, sure. It's rock and roll, isn't it?

What they never mention, the elitist snobs, the impudent rapscallions, the no-good filthy snot-dripping bastards, is that bubblegum derived from the raw, wounded Delta blues sung by the young grand-children of Leadbelly and Howlin' Wolf, combined with the premodern narrative power of Mother Goose. Or that bubblegum in its turn helped give rise to hip-hop, Britney Spears, *Teen People* magazine, the Doobie Brothers, and the comedy of Adam Sandler.

Another positive thing that can be said (and will, as long as I have one last breath in my body) about bubblegum is that while many rock bands deliberately sing lyrics that are lightly disguised paeans to drugs, bubblegum groups sang lyrics that were lightly disguised paeans to sweets. Though it is true that candy, gum, pastry, and root beer can be addictive and cause alarming weight gain and tooth decay, their effects are hardly as disruptive to society as those of smack or crack.

Consider, for example, these lyrics from the Archies' 1969 megahit, "Sugar, Sugar":

Unsuccessful as a Beatles tribute band, Genghis Khan's Pony switched to bubblegum and topped the Mongolian charts in 1977 with "Have a Jujube, Judy."

Pour a little sugar on it, oh yeah
Pour a little sugar on it, honey
Pour a little sugar on it, baby

We are not concerned here with the explicit meaning of this passage, which is clearly obscene, but rather the subtext. The subtle repetition of "sugar" and the additional use of "honey" subliminally entice the listener to desire sweet foods, to procure them, and to stuff them down his or her gaping maw until he or she pukes.

In fact, I think I'll take a break from writing this right now and get myself a Hershey bar.

Damn, that was good. Wish I had another.

The Archies were, of course, one of those groups that had no evident human component, being, as they were, a television cartoon derived from a comic strip. At the time, some people did believe that Archie, Jughead, Reggie, Veronica, and Betty were singing and playing the group's hits, but these people were soon hunted down by white-jacketed men wielding butterfly nets and put away where they couldn't hurt anyone.

Most of the anonymous session musicians who actually created the Archies' sound later suffered from serious mental problems including flashbacks, depression, fear of sudden noises, and a tendency to make loud popping sounds with their mouth parts even when not chewing gum.

Inane rhyming and mindless repetition of key words (particularly words ending in the letter Y) were important ingredients of the bubblegum formula that flooded the AM airwaves with hits in the late '60s and early '70s before the entire genre was swept away by a nasty scandal involving the deaths of numerous musicians and toddler-aged fans from sucrose overdoses. Such hits included "Jingle Jangle" and "Bang-Shang-a-Lang" by the Archies and "Yummy Yummy Yummy" and "Chewy Chewy" by the Ohio Express, as well as "Goody Goody Gumdrop" by the 1910 Fruitgum Company, "Licky Licky Lollipop" by Big Daddy and the Sucking Candies, and "Gummy Gummy" by the American Dentifrice Manufacturers' Association.

Before bubblegum plummeted to its inevitable doom, leaving a bitter taste in the nation's mouth, it endured a brief but intense spate of hybridization. Perhaps the most unfortunate of these derivative subgenres was bubblebilly, a style typified by Bobby Carl Pinkett's filthy 1972 song, "Who Licked All the Cream Outta My Gol-Dern Twinkies?" However, some would argue that an even worse offshoot was heavy bubble, as personified by the group Clown, which incited a riot at its first and last concert at Boston's Fenway Park when the six heavily made-up and costumed band members climbed out of a guitar case, sprayed the audience with seltzer, and smashed their instruments over each others' heads *before* playing their songs.

Greatest Unknown Songs of the Classic Bubblegum Era (1967-1975)	
Dum Dum	Carrot Tree
Hazy Hazy	Bubbles
Sticky, Sticky	1910 Fruitgum Company
Hunky Funky	American Breed
Jingle Jangle	The Archies
Yummy Yummy Yummy	Candy Rock Generation
Oopy-Doopy-Sam	Kiwis
Da-Da-Da-Da	Changing Colours
Ooo-Chee Boo-Chee	Bourbon Family
Chirpy Chirpy Cheep Cheep	Lally Stott
Ricky Ticky Ta Ta Ta	Austin Roberts
Lotti Lotti/Loop De Loop	Blizzard
Dong-Dong-Diki-Di-Ki-Dong	Kasenetz Super Cirkus
Tweedelee Dee	Avengers
Polly-Wally-Doo-Da-Day	1910 Fruitgum Company
Fee-Fi-Fo-Fum	Hungry Tiger
Coochie Coochie Coo	Hudson Brothers
Eeny Meeny Miny Moe	Luv
Wham! Bam! Ala Cazam	Tricks
Ah-La	Fighter Squadron
Sha La La	Zoot
Sha-La Love	Uniques
Sha-La-La-La-La	Walkers
Shaka Shaka Na Na	Countdown Five

Chapter 35   THE '80S: BRIDGE TO NOWHERE

It has been suggested by some experts that we are still too close to the 1980s to be able to undertake an accurate assessment of the musical landscape of that era, with its extreme fragmentation, its lack of obvious mainstream trends, its paucity of rock giants and originals, and its yellow polka-dot neckties.

Ha! You call those experts? What a bunch of cowards! Come on, take a position! This is a no-brainer. It's simple. The '80s were the decade when rock and roll finally died. As I have hinted earlier, rock started to run out of gas in the mid-'70s. By the '80s, everything interesting had been done, the corporations had reasserted control over the music, and the expressions of rage, danger, and rebellion fueling the best rock and roll had withered into empty ritual. Rock and roll—indeed, all popular music—indeed, all life on earth—was a hollow shell, a mere remnant of something once vital and dynamic, a shell of a husk of a pod with no cream-filled center, no nougat or caramel, no beating heart, no soul, no nothing.

Is this depressing or what?

Really, if I had any integrity at all, I would end the book right here. Just have a bunch of blank pages after this one. But my publisher says such a course of action would be unwise for two reasons:

1. It would put off younger readers, who actually think—and I personally find this hard to believe but the publisher insists it's true—that some of the recent stuff is okay.

2. He, that is, the publisher, would sue my ass.

So the beat goes on.

But I warn you. From here on out, things are going to get grim. Our story becomes one of entropy, enuresis (don't look it up—you don't want to know), lack of authenticity, and lethargy. It's like one of those appalling poems by Yeats or Eliot that despair of modern life, all full of hollow men and things falling apart and rough beasts slouching toward Bethlehem to be born. Which, come to think of it, would make a pretty good hook for a heavy-metal lyric.

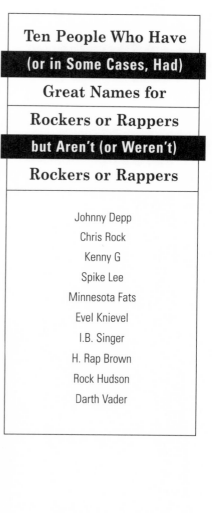

Ten People Who Have (or in Some Cases, Had) Great Names for Rockers or Rappers but Aren't (or Weren't) Rockers or Rappers

Johnny Depp
Chris Rock
Kenny G
Spike Lee
Minnesota Fats
Evel Knievel
I.B. Singer
H. Rap Brown
Rock Hudson
Darth Vader

Forensic investigators gather to study the corpse of rock and roll.

Chapter 36

THE AMAZING STORY OF MTV, THE REVOLUTION IT BROUGHT TO AMERICAN LIFE AND THE FORTUNE IT MADE FOR A SMALL GROUP OF BALD, FAT, CORPORATE EXECUTIVES IN VERY EXPENSIVE ITALIAN SUITS DESIGNED TO CONCEAL THEIR OBSCENELY BULGING PAUNCHES

Ever since the dawn of television, men (and the occasional woman or child) had dreamed of squeezing rock and roll inside a TV set.

As we have noted in earlier, more energetic chapters, broadcast pioneers like Dick Clark, Ed Sullivan, and Captain Kangaroo had tried valiantly to do so. But televising a live band playing live music before a live audience (or, in the case of Sullivan, a half-dead audience), while thrilling and sexually stimulating to the backward viewers of the mid-twentieth century, was a crude, laborious process that wasted vast amounts of energy and polluted the environment.

Something new was needed, something utilizing innovative technology borrowed from the space program and revolutionary cultural ideas that could turn all established laws and customs upside down. That something came along in 1981. It was called MTV.

MTV was the brainchild of Moreland C. Nethercutt, an artificial-flavor engineer for Kraft Foods who, while on holiday in Bulgaria, had seen something called a music video on an obscure government cable-television channel. He sped back to corporate headquarters and excitedly filed a memo alerting top company officials to, in his words, "Forget processed cheese. We can make billions on music videos!" Like all great visionaries, Nethercutt was immediately fired and committed by his family to a mental hospital.

Several years later, his idea was stolen by Warner Entertainment and American Express, which launched MTV on a tiny investment of twenty million dollars. It was only after the channel debuted that panicked company executives realized there were no music videos in existence yet, except for the primitive ones on that station in Bulgaria, which mainly involved accordions and tractors, a

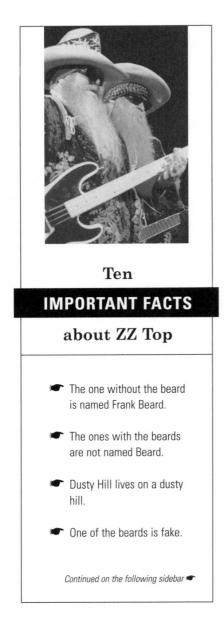

Ten

IMPORTANT FACTS

about ZZ Top

- ☞ The one without the beard is named Frank Beard.

- ☞ The ones with the beards are not named Beard.

- ☞ Dusty Hill lives on a dusty hill.

- ☞ One of the beards is fake.

Continued on the following sidebar ☞

148

---

combination unlikely to appeal to American fans, except possibly those who liked country music.

Thinking quickly, MTV's president, a failed squirrel-feed salesman named Ken Lay, sent out a camera crew with strict, detailed instructions to grab the first rock band they came across, throw some weird costumes on them and tape them running around and doing zany, picturesque things.

The band chosen was Roberto Duran, an English group that had been expelled from Britain for founding the Gloved Romantic movement, which combined disco and boxing. Due to a misprint on a teleprompter and an overstimulated "veejay," as MTV's hosts were known, the band was introduced to viewers as "Duran! Duran!" and the name stuck. Flocking to the new channel by the millions while abandoning school, work, and military commitments, American teenagers and young adults quickly made Duran Duran the hottest act in the country and its pretty-boy lead singer, Simon LeBon, the biggest pain in the ass.

MTV was on its way to glory. Having once tasted the sweet elixir of success, its executives wanted more, more, MORE! They inundated radio and television with a clever commercial featuring various celebrities screaming the catchy slogan, "I want my MTV. Whether you get your MTV I couldn't care less. It's all about me."

In addition to Duran Duran, early MTV featured a number of British groups with French names such as Depeche Mode and Nous Sommes Merde. They dressed as Restoration fops or Aztec priests in their slickly produced videos featuring scantily clad women, exotic zoo animals, and fast bicycles and they produced an "electro-pop" sound utilizing electronic synthesizers, drum machines, and Waring blenders. As these instruments did not require the presence of any human beings, they were highly popular among musicians who yearned to be rock stars but could not play. Inevitably, such conditions led to the infamous Milli Vanilli scandal (covered in revolting detail in the next chapter), which would have brought down the entire music industry had anyone paid it the slightest attention.

Another techno-pop group that became popular was Roxy Music, cofounded by Brian Eno, for whom fate and a short name would secure a place as the man appearing in more crossword puzzles than any music star since Yma Sumac ("Yma, meet Uma," as David Letterman once said), with her famous 18-octave range.

MTV's growing popularity could be measured in the impressive statistics compiled by the U.S. Bureau of Meaningless Numbers. By 1983, the channel reached seventeen million homes, attracted viewers with an average age of 23, consumed 6.8 million hamburgers a week, and, if laid end to end, would stretch from Tokyo, Japan, to the planet Pluto.

But MTV was not to everyone's taste. Some critics found it excessively salty. Others argued that MTV shortened attention spans, rewarded beauty and visual sparkle above talent, robbed artists of their mystery, objectified women, glorified violence, promoted decadence, pacified the TV audience, stifled spontaneity, stunted the imagination, erased the boundaries between creativity and commercialism, and dumped hundreds of tons of hydrocarbons into the world's oceans every year. All these charges were true but

- Before calling itself ZZ Top, the band played under the name the Two Bearded Guys and Their Clean-Shaven Buddy.

- On the Worldwide Texas Tour in 1970, the band had snakes, longhorn cattle, buffalo, armadillos, centipedes, scorpions, cactus plants, and dead mules onstage with them. The smell was overpowering.

- Pledged in 1991 to keep growing their beards until kissed by England's Prince William.

- Admitted in 1983 to having been strongly influenced by the Smith Brothers of cough-drop fame.

- First band to use a name starting with double Zs.

- All their songs sound alike.

no one cared except a few carping intellectuals and they were soon set upon, beaten up, slathered with hot tar, and lashed naked to stakes in the desert to be devoured by army ants because we, the people, were sick and tired of their constant whining and pretending to be better than everyone else.

For truly, MTV had changed the landscape, not only in music, but all the popular arts. Network television dramas began to ape the MTV hallmarks of bright pastel colors, quick editing cuts, and total disregard for logical plot progression or narrative (innovations that I have gratefully borrowed for use in this book). Radio DJs now played mainly musicians featured on MTV. Philharmonic orchestras added synthesizers and veejays. Abstract expressionists dripped paint on their TV screens. Two members of ZZ Top grew long beards to add visual interest to their act. Eventually, a man from Texas with no intellectual curiosity, a disdain for scientific research, and an inability to speak English was twice chosen President of the United States.

MTV had revolutionized the world. And Bulgaria had ruined everything once again.

Chapter 37

MILLI VANILLI WAS A DILLI. RILLI!

by guest author Jayson Blair

It was the best of times, it was the worst of times. The '80s. Ah, yes, I remember them well. You wore blue; the Germans wore glitter. They were trying to imitate the British, who were then in the throes of glam. That's where Milli Vanilli began, in Düsseldorf, the leading industrial city of East Germany, famed for the manufacture of tungsten ore.

I'll never forget the first time I saw Milli Vanilli. I was chief European correspondent for the *New York Times*, a very prestigious position and one never before occupied by a feisty young black man with both brains and sex appeal.

Only two months before, I had graduated summa cum magnum from the Harvard School of Journalism and impressed *Times* executive editor Howell Raines with my confidence, intellect, and charm. "Jayson," he told me, calling me by name, an unprecedented honor for a young job applicant, "I want you to cover Europe for the *Times*. Sure, it's outrageous to give such a post to someone just out of college. But the people we have there now just don't get it. They're too conventional; they're tired hacks. If our readers can just see the continent through your eyes, from the perspective of a charming, intelligent young black man of immense talent and physical beauty, then by God, we shall add half a dozen Pulitzers to our already brimming trophy case."

So there I was in Düsseldorf, covering a summit meeting of all the crowned heads of Europe. At night, I would "do the town" with my friend Catherine Deneuve, the fantastically beautiful French

Driven from Europe by scandal, an increasingly desperate Milli Vanilli try to pass themselves off as Bob Dylan and Willie Nelson. Few are fooled.

movie star (I really dig older babes!), whom I'd been "seeing," if you catch my drift, whenever I was in Paris and who often followed me to other cities.

One night we went to the secret mountaintop hideaway of German Chancellor Hans von Wiener Schnitzel for an intimate late supper of sauerbraten with sauerkraut cooked by Hans's voluptuous mistress Helga. (I'd had a thing with her before she met Hans.) After this delicious repast, we sipped schnapps and talked late into the night of many things: European politics, the films of Chevy Chase, and the books of Kitty Kelley. And then Hans said he had a special treat for us. The lights went down and when they came up again, there stood two men, Milton (Milli) Martin and Bill Vanilli.

They sang, they danced, they told jokes, they did ventriloquism (with Vanilli sitting in Milli's lap)—and it was magical, a throwback to the old days of decadent Weimar cabaret before the Nazis came and wiped out the Liza Minnellis of the world. We were up until the rosy-fingered dawn crept over the wine-dark sea, regaled by that wonderful duo and their tight backup band, das Rollink Schtönes.

So it was no surprise to me when soon afterward MV exploded into international stardom, their albums blazing to the tops of even the highest charts. Who among my generation will ever forget the songs of Milli Vanilli? "Girl You Know It's True" and "Girl I'm Gonna Miss You" and "Baby Don't Forget My Number" are songs you still hear everywhere today, and no wonder. They say everything that needs to be said about girls and truth and numbers.

You can imagine how shocked, nay, how devastated I was to hear the false charges that were suddenly thrown at MV at the very peak of their greatness. Didn't write their songs? Didn't even sing their own songs? Weren't wearing their own underwear? What a pack of lies. Of course, it was nothing but jealousy. All the bitter, no-talent burnouts in the industry, the people who envied the success of these two upstarts, wanted to bring them down, just the way they wanted to bring me down. Despite the racial progress that has been made in the music industry, the white establishment still couldn't abide the idea of an act loved by smart young black men like me becoming the biggest superstars of all time.

So down they went. What happened to Milli Vanilli was disgraceful, a mark of shame against our so-called civilization. (Ha! What a laugh.) When will we ever learn, is what I want to know. And where have all the flowers gone? Gone for soldiers, every one. And so we beat on, boats against the current, borne back ceaselessly into the past. But still, despite everything, I remain an optimist. I mean, what the hell. I've lived a life that's full. I've traveled each and every highway. But more, much more than this, I did it my way.

So it goes.

People Who Think They're Rock Stars but Aren't

| Bill Clinton | Howard Stern | Barry Manilow | Jann Wenner | Louis XIV |

Chapter 38

THE MAN WHO MADE NEW JERSEY FAMOUS

For centuries, the marshy area between New York, Pennsylvania, Delaware, and the Atlantic Ocean lay in a forgotten state. The state of New Jersey. Nothing ever happened there and it smelled bad. The only famous person who ever lived in New Jersey for any amount of time was Albert Einstein and he had to be imported from Germany and bribed to remain at Princeton. Frank Sinatra was born in Hoboken but left as soon as he was old enough to sneak on the ferry to New York. Even Jersey cows were snubbed by Holsteins and Guernseys. And football jerseys were looked down on by polo shirts. The state's best-known feature was the New Jersey Turnpike and that was designed to get you through the place as quickly as possible. Then in 1949, everything changed. Bruce was born.

Bruuuuuuuuuuuuuuuuuuuuuuuuuuuce! [1]

Bruce, whose real name was Springsteen, had the good fortune to be born and raised near the Jersey Shore, an area strikingly similar to a beach, though not as cute. Asbury Park, where Bruce hung out whenever he could, was a sleazy, shabby, seedy, sordid, squalid, dead-end dump for derelicts, do-nothings, dimwits, down-and-outers, and deadwood…in other words, a typical twentieth-century American town full of ordinary folk whose crushed hopes and miserable disappointments Bruce could immortalize in provocative, poignant, poetic songs that would penetrate straight to the heart, causing severe bleeding in the left ventricle.

---

1. That was the sound of millions of you readers yelling "Bruce!" all at once.

Had he been born in Grosse Point, Michigan, or Beverly Hills, California, he never would have amounted to a damn thing.

But first he had to grow up, learn to play the guitar, and struggle through dozens of lame garage bands and incompetent sidemen, which is nature's way of weeding the weak, the unfit, and the crabgrassical out of the lush, perfumed garden of stardom.[2] Also, the young Bruce had to lose a disturbing tendency to write songs sounding like those of the god of folk-rock so that he would not be mistaken for just another Dylantante.

Lyrics committed under the influence such as "Hey, Mr. Tanned Machine Man, pray along with me; in the Jersey City morning, I'll come wallowing, too" seemed embarrassing after the passage of time—say, three minutes.

Ultimately it was the romanticism of Bruce, rooted in the idealism of the '60s but tempered by the disillusionment of the '70s, '30s, '40s, '50s, and '90s (like all the great ones, Bruce was prophetic) that carried him to superstardom in the '80s. That romanticism appealed to the tragically aging baby boomers who had protested against the Vietnam War in the '60s and now missed it desperately.

In 1973, Bruce formed the soon-to-be-famous E Street Band, named for the only paved street in Ho-Ho-Kus, New Jersey. It was the next year, by most accounts 1974, that the influential foreign rock correspondent Jon Landau saw the band play at a small club in Mongolia and penned his now-legendary line in the underground paper the *Christian Science Monitor:* "I have seen the future of rock and roll and its name is Bryce Springstern."

This drummer auditioned for the E Street Band but was rejected because Bruce Springsteen detested argyle kneesocks.

2. I had a few botanical metaphors left over from the flower-power chapter so I thought I'd work one in here.

Though Jon Bon Jovi hailed from the same state as Bruce Springsteen, that doesn't necessarily mean they are related. A lot of people make this mistake. There is also much confusion arising from the fact that Bon Jovi is both the name of Jon Bon Jovi's band, Bon Jovi, and Bon Jovi's lead singer, Jon Bon Jovi, though not the real name of either. Bon Jovi the person was born Jove Ben Jovius but an evil manager made him change it because it sounded too ancient Roman/Hebrew. Bon Jovi's pop-metal sound, so reminiscent of Jersey swamp gas, made it one of the dominant mainstream rock bands of the '80s, which is not to say that it was any good. One of Bon Jovi's great innovations, introduced on the 1986

Continued on the following sidebar ☛

The fact that Landau had written the same thing about Grand Funk Railroad, Engelbert Humperdinck, Grace Jones, the Association, the Bonzo Dog Band, and Dino, Desi, and Billy bothered no one because, as Samuel Johnson often wrote, hey, when you're right, you're right. Bruce's career plummeted to new heights of glory. So did Landau's when Bruce appointed him producer, manager, and massage therapist for the E Street Band.

The result of their collaboration was Bruce's breakthrough album, *Born on the Run*, which celebrated the joys of jogging. "I was 24 and sick and tired of writing songs about girls and cars," Bruce later told Diane Sawyer on the ABC show Nightsweat. "So instead I wrote about jogging with girls and running after cars." Although no one bought the album, there was much discussion about it in the barbershops and diners of the land and Bruce made the covers of both *Time* and *Newsweek*, which were then experiencing their slowest week for news in thirty years. After that, everyone knew Bruce was famous even if they had never heard of him.

As Bruce surged into his all-important thirties, his lyrics dealt increasingly with the alienation, isolation, breakdown of values, cynicism, spiritual poverty, and intellectual bankruptcy that had always been such indispensable attributes of life in America, though his tunes remained bravely upbeat and bouncy. The poignant "Parking Lot Blues," for example, told the tale of a former high-school football hero who loses his job when he runs over the boss's daughter in the parking lot of the steel mill where he works, breaking her collarbone. He then drinks himself to death, scribbling a poignant suicide note requesting everyone in the bleak heartland of industrial Middle America to "please go fuck yourselves, not that I want you to feel guilty or anything."

As his vision darkened, Bruce found himself facing an existential crisis that did not let up until he remembered to take off his sunglasses. His masterful 1984 album *Bored with the USA* won over even the jingoistic rubes of the right, who mistook his disgust with them for rabid patriotic fervor, linguistic acumen not being their forte. They led the cheers that drowned out Bruce's band throughout its Bored tour as Bruce-O-Mania swept the nation, the planet, and then the solar system, causing tsunamis in the Martian canals.

Bruce became so popular that he got his own nickname, the Boss, although not until after a nasty fight with New York Yankees owner George Steinbrenner, who claimed that he owned all rights to the tag, having purchased it from the late Mayor Richard Daley of Chicago, who had inherited it directly from New York's William Marcy Tweed.

Unfortunately, Bruce's personal life was not as turmoil-roiled as his music, hurting his stature as a major rock deity. He seldom collapsed from drug overdoses, was hardly ever arrested, and suffered only one divorce, from a generic model/actress who was, after all, of a different gender than he. He then decided to marry one of the members of his E Street Band. Ultimately it came down to a choice between Patti Scialfa and "Little Steven" Van Zandt. After several agonizing minutes, he chose Big Patti. Heartbroken, Van Zandt joined the Mafia, becoming an underboss to New Jersey capo Tony Soprano. Whatever Van Zandt did, it had to have some connection to music.

album *Slippery When Wet*, was letting fans pick the songs. Tapes of thirty possible tunes were played for a jury of teenagers, who rejected all thirty and wrote their own. The album sold nine million copies. The band broke up in 1987, got back together in 1988, broke up again in 1999, reformed in 2000, fell down and broke its hips in 2001, and was declared obsolete in 2002. In 2003, an anthology album, *The Best of Bon Jovi*, was released and in 2004, another anthology album, *The Return of the Best of Bon Jovi,* was released. In 2005, both were recalled as safety hazards.

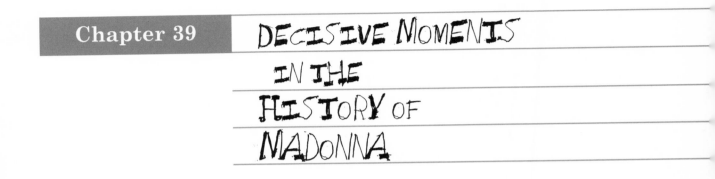

Chapter 39

DECISIVE MOMENTS IN THE HISTORY OF MADONNA

August 16, 1958:

Madonna Louise Veronica Ciccone is born in Bay City, Michigan. She immediately calls a press conference to announce her arrival.

September 20, 1963:

Upon entering kindergarten, Madonna drops three of her names, declaring that henceforth she will be known simply as "Ciccone." Later, she will rethink this hasty decision.

February 12, 1966:

Madonna redefines the nature of elementary-school eroticism when she briefly lifts her hoop skirt and flashes her underpants while portraying Mary Todd Lincoln in the third grade's annual President's Day Pageant. Though the principal faints, the fifth-grade boys are visibly aroused and several begin growing beards the same week.

September 12, 1972:

Now calling herself simply "Veronica," Madonna graduates from high school and enrolls in the University of Michigan, where she majors in image engineering with a minor in postmodern irony.

April 3, 1978:

Moving to New York with only three dollars in her training bustier, Madonna sets out to begin her show-business career after spotting a help-wanted ad in *Variety* for an entry-level position as a megastar trainee.

April 4, 1979:

Realizing that her dark tresses are preventing her from being promoted to blond bombshell, Madonna bleaches her hair for the first time and finds it a thrilling, life-changing experience.

July 16, 1980:

After being expelled from the Alvin Ailey Dance Theater for picking up guys at the barre, Madonna begins frequenting downtown discos and clubs. There she develops an attention-getting look combining lacy underwear and bejeweled crucifixes. This attracts her a horde of conflicted admirers desiring to take her home to meet Mom and then ravish her on the kitchen table.

August 12, 1980:

A boyfriend lets Madonna sing and play drums in his band, often simultaneously. So eager is Madonna to make good, she frequently continues singing and playing even after the other band members have gone home and the club has closed,

Always health-conscious, Madonna gives herself a breast exam as Death looks on during a break in the filming of her 1984 remake of Ingmar Bergman's *The Seventh Seal* as a musical.

January 29, 1981:

Madonna gains admittance to the ultra-trendy downtown club Danceteria by agreeing to start three new trends a year. Making good on her promise, she invents techno-punk music, e-mail, and cleaning up after your dog poops.

February 9, 1982:

Madonna records her first album, *Madonna*. Its songs are played incessantly on MTV, launching her into national stardom. But national stardom is not enough, so Madonna begins studying Spanish, French, German, Chinese, Swahili, and Serbo-Croatian.

February 16, 1983:

In a career-making epiphany, Madonna decides she will stay on top by constantly reinventing herself, changing her image with each new album, movie, or surge of hormones. In the space of only three weeks, she tries out the Aztec look, the forest-ranger look, and the Little Miss Muffet look.

January 28, 1984:

Madonna releases her breakthrough album *Like a Virgin*, despite the severe mental strain she suffers trying to remember what it was like.

May 3, 1985:

Madonna introduces the phrase "Boy Toy" into the English language, wearing the words on her belt buckle during an MTV awards show. She becomes the first singer of her generation to appear both on MTV and in the *Oxford English Dictionary*.

August 16, 1985:

Madonna weds combustible actor Sean Penn. The marriage is stopped in the first round with Madonna declared the winner on a TKO.

October 16, 1986:

Shanghai Surprise, starring Madonna and Penn, debuts. It is hailed by critics as the worst film of the year and, for good measure, the next year as well.

December 18, 1986:

Madonna releases the hit song "Papa Don't Preach," but her father refuses to give up his Sunday sermons and is finally arrested for impersonating a priest.

April 5, 1987:

Unveiling yet another new image in the film *Who's That Girl*, Madonna shows off her new punk look, wearing spiky platinum hair and huge muscles borrowed for the occasion from the Incredible Hulk. The film establishes Madonna as a movie star of a magnitude comparable only to Ben Affleck's.

May 3, 1988:

Madonna makes her Broadway acting debut in the title role of David Mamet's *Speed-the-Plow*. The critics pan it (using real pans) but audiences applaud politely, leaving the theater with a slightly puzzled look.

June 1, 1989:

Madonna's "Like a Prayer" video, featuring burning crosses and an eroticized black Jesus, is attacked by the Vatican, which claims that the real Jesus did not dance to rock music. Fortunately, polls show that 63 percent of the American public believe Madonna's version is the more accurate one.

September 20, 1990:

Madonna stars with joke boyfriend Warren Beatty in *Dick Tracy*, playing Breathless Mahoney, a nightclub singer who likes Dick. Rumors of a Madonna-Beatty affair cause panic among America's senior citizens, who fear that rough sex between the two could cause the demise of the superannuated leading man.

Ol' Madonna
Had a Clone

There have been many rock and pop tribute bands, from Björn Again, the Abba impersonators out of Australia, to ZZ Bottom, the gay ZZ Top doppelgangers from Norway who wear their fake beards in the wrong places. There are more than 12,500 performers listed in the International Registry of Elvis Impersonators and an estimated 500 bands around the world pretending to be the Beatles. But no doubt the most original tribute band is Mad Donna, the ever-expanding troupe of Madonna imitators, each of whom portrays the superstar in a different phase of her career. "We're up to 37 members now," says Stu Blenheim, who specializes in the downtown-Manhattan Madonna of the *Desperately Seeking Susan* era. "If Madonna reinvents herself another couple of times, our act is gonna be six hours long."

September 9, 1991:

In her backstage film documentary *Truth or Dare*, Madonna again breaks all the rules and causes a furor, this time by appearing with her clothes on.

November 5, 1992:

Madonna affirms her business acumen by signing a multimillion-dollar deal with Time Warner, giving her full control of all the money in her checking account.

April 30, 1996:

Starring in the world's longest music video, *Evita*, Madonna brilliantly portrays Argentine pop star Eva Peron, wowing movie audiences with her rendition of such Andrew Lloyd Webber hits as "Don't Laugh at Me, Argentina, or I'll Have Juan Give You a Smack Upside the Head" and the poignant ballad "Che, I Think You're in the Wrong Movie."

October 14, 1996:

Madonna has her first child, a girl, named Lourdes. It is believed to be a non-virgin birth.

August 8, 1999:

Madonna appears to be over.

October 3, 1999:

Madonna is not over!

May 1, 2000:

Madonna moves to London and begins taking British-accent lessons. Soon she sounds so British, Queen Elizabeth mistakes her for a member of the Royal Family and gives her a small castle. Madonna complains to the media that what she really wanted was to be dubbed Duke of Earl.

December 22, 2000:

Madonna marries Guy Ritchie, director of the acclaimed gangster film *I'll Kill You, You No-Good, Stinking Motherfucker. Oh Yeah? You and What Army?* Three thousand guests attend the wedding at Westminster Abbey, including Sting, the archbishop of Canterbury, Stephen Hawking, and Princess Diana, who receives special leave from heaven for the occasion.

September 11, 2001:

An airliner hijacked by Muslim terrorists is unable to locate its primary target, Madonna, and goes on to strike one of the World Trade Center towers.

August 23, 2003:

Madonna makes a tongue-in-cheek appearance at the MTV Music Awards, the cheek belonging to Britney Spears.

September 6, 2003:

Madonna begins teaching a seminar at Harvard Business School in image engineering and postmodern irony.

December 18, 2003:

Madonna begins studying the ancient Jewish mystical lore known as Kabbalah and is given the spiritual name Esther Slansky.

May 12, 2004:

While intoning an ancient Jewish mystical chant, Madonna mispronounces a crucial Aramaic gerund and inadvertently summons a small dybbuk who becomes painfully lodged in her pupik. This necessitates a dangerous ancient mystical ritual known as a pupikectomy, which Madonna miraculously survives.

August 3, 2005:

Israeli Premier Ariel Sharon announces that Israel Defense Forces have begun building a fence around Madonna to protect her from terrorist attack.

September 17, 2006:

In her ultimate reinvention, Madonna tours sixteen countries as a gigantic, edible eggplant. Scientists are mystified over how she achieved the startling transformation.

Chapter 40

UNDER THE MICHAELSCOPE

(In Which the Cream of Academe

Pores Over the King of Pop)

In November, 2003, a three-day interdisciplinary academic symposium was held at England's Oxford University. Some 400 distinguished scholars from around the globe convened to discuss a topic of urgent import: "Michael Jackson: What's With Him, Anyway?" Here are excerpts from some of the papers presented that were judged Best in Show.

Dr. Alvin J. Wanzell,
professor of advanced media studies at Florida State University:

Let us not, I submit, fall into the category error of focusing fixedly on the contemporary Jackson persona, with its unfortunate intimations of pedophilia, but rather on the performance skills of the mega-entertainer who once danced, sang, and seized the genital area (his own, which is legal) with astounding vitality and grace. What a loss to society. This performer's unique physical appearance, piping castrato voice, and effortless terpsichorean levitations were so unearthly as to be divine. Indeed, the overall effect was of a kind that could only be measured by what Baudrillard referred to as "hyper-real incandescence." By which I mean, to put it in layman's idiom, Michael Jackson was just so fucking weird, you couldn't take your eyes off him.

Dr. Chen Dweng, chairman,
Department of Internal Phrenology, University of Beijing:

My study reveals that most of Michael Jackson's emotional problems stem from the prepubescent phase, when his parents paid insufficient attention to feng shui in the family domicile in Gary, Indiana. For instance, Jackson's bedroom door directly faced the bathroom. As any first-year graduate student knows, this generates negative chi from the toilet—unless one hangs a wind chime outside the bedroom door or displays a crystal globe (first soaked in rock-salt water for seven days) near the child to dissipate the injurious chi waves. Tragically, neither precaution was taken.

Furthermore, the father, Joseph Jackson, failed to secure the yang energy in the paternal sector, or northwestern portion, of the home. This blunder permitted a severe imbalance in the domicile's force field, dooming its juvenile occupants to dreadful love luck for the rest of their lives. Had the father simply repainted the entire northwest sector a bright red and closed all the windows, thus keeping out water chi and insect energy, it is likely that Michael Jackson would have grown up filial, obedient, and a credit to the family instead of the far-fetched lunatic he has become.

Dr. Hildegard Minth,
director of women's studies, U.S. Military Academy at West Point:

I submit to you that the root of Michael's difficulty in differentiating reality from fantasy is that he sees his penis as a phallic symbol instead of an actual penis.

Dr. Owen C. Bergenthaler,
professor of mechanical psychology, University of California at Buffalo:

Many of my colleagues have postulated that in his psychosexual maturation, Michael Jackson failed to progress beyond the prepubescent stage and remains in a permanent state of arrested development, thus explaining his need to surround himself with toys, exotic pets, young children,

Asked how many years he's spent in plastic surgery and how many feet high his fake afro is, Michael Jackson thinks quickly.

and fudge; to adorn himself in silly costumes; and to speak in the voice of an eight-year-old. There is, however, an alternate possibility, namely, that during the 1980s, when Jackson famously slept in a hyperbaric-oxygen chamber in an attempt to extend his life beyond its natural span, something may have gone horribly awry. Experiments conducted in my laboratory show that even a slight error in the chamber's settings can result in exactly the symptoms exhibited by our subject. Furthermore, due to the absorption of oxygen under high pressure into his lymphatic system, he remains even now in grave danger of exploding any time he ventures near an electrical source. (He has already exploded once, during the filming of a soft-drink commercial. The second time could prove fatal not only to him, but to thousands of people in the immediate vicinity.) If my theory is correct, he should be rushed to a hospital immediately and submit to the administration of a plutonium enema before he is transformed into a tiny, smoking mound of ash. This procedure will not only obviate any danger of detonation but quickly restore Michael Jackson to complete normalcy, the only side effect being that he will then display all the outward characteristics of a man 150 years old.

Dr. Ludovico Vermicelli,
professor emeritus of advanced semiotic theory,
University of Bulgaria at Plotsk.

In 1717, anticipating the power of television and cinema 250 years later, the philosopher George Berkeley formulated his famous principle *esse est percipi*, "To be is to be perceived." Perhaps, but is the reverse also true? That is to say, just because we have seen Michael Jackson on a screen or read about him in a newspaper, how can we be certain he really exists? As the old aphorism has it, "If God did not exist, we would have to invent him." I would propound the thesis that the same is true of Michael Jackson, that this iconic persona prancing so vividly before us is nothing more than a kind of mass hallucination that all of us in Western Civilization have unknowingly conspired to create. In short, he is no more than a transcendental signifier. Ah, you say, but if so, what does he signify? Here we arrive at the crux of the matter. Yet, painfully, I must confess that I haven't the foggiest idea what he signifies. I don't know, maybe I'm just not as smart as I thought I was when I commenced this analysis. I'm *pretty* smart, sure, but I'm no Einstein. Frankly, this intractable issue has catapulted me into a crisis of conscience. Perhaps I should resign my prestigious and amply compensated post. Such a course of action would plunge me into a depression the likes of which I have never known and probably result in suicide. But if it is the right thing to do, ethically I have no other choice. Please, you must help me.

Dr. Marvin Steele Finklestein,
Charles Van Doren Fellow, Institute of Higher Thinking,
Palo Alto, California.

Well, I know what he signifies because I am breathtakingly smart. I have an IQ of 273, I'm vice president of Mensa, and I can multiply large sums in my head without recourse to a calculator. Now then, looking at the case history of our subject though the

---

Most Popular Exhibits, Boutiques, and Rides at the Rock and Roll HALL OF FAME and the Adjoining ROCK ADVENTURE PARK

- Tomb of the Unknown Groupie
- Pirated CDs of the Caribbean
- Elton's Designer Optical Salon
- Mummified Remains of Keith Richards
- Animatronic Jim Morrison Exhibitionism Exhibit
- Woodstock Mud Wallow
- Michael Jackson's Haunted Castle of Horrors (Free admission for boys under 15)
- P. Diddy's Rap Karaoke Bar
- Doc Leary's Old-Fashioned Travelin' Pharmacy
- Proud Mary's Riverboat Adventure
- Cheech & Chong's Highly Scientifical Agriculture Project
- Buddy Holly's Cockpit Simulator
- Ex-Pips vs. Ex-Vandellas Tag-Team Wrestling Show
- Guess-Dick-Clark's-Age Booth
- Britney's Vegas Wedding Chapel
- Courtney Love's Descent-into-Hell Ride
- Tupac's Shootin' Gallery
- Gene Simmons's Tongue-Kissing Booth

perspective of history, we quickly come to realize that his downfall, if downfall it is—never rule out a show-biz comeback!—is bigger than one individual's misfortune. It is nothing less than the tragedy of a nation, if not civilization itself, for Michael Jackson symbolizes, indeed, embodies, the United States of America, a once-great country, the world's only superpower though now corroded to the very core of its fiber by greed, sloth, political and corporate corruption, sexual depravity, and moral putrefaction. And I say to you, brothers and sisters, I say, Repent! Repent before it is too late! For the Lord waxes wroth and if we do not repent, surely He will bring down upon us fire and brimstone and plagues of vermin! Get down on your knees and pray, ye blasphemous heathens! Right now! Get down! Pray! Repent!

OK, just kidding. Everyone up. This symposium was getting kind of dull so I thought I'd liven things up a bit. A little pedagogical humor there! Is it time for lunch yet, Mr. Chairman? I don't know about you but I could ingest an equine.

Chapter 41

The Chapter Formerly Known as Prince

He was born a Prince but he died a common rock star. [1]

His name at birth was Prince Rogers William Madonna Lord Horatio Nelson. But he outgrew all that verbiage to become simply the Artist Formerly Known as an Unpronounceable Symbol. And yet, most people just call him "that wacky Prince."

Interestingly, he was born in Minnesota, the same state as Bob Dylan, a fact that holds no significance whatsoever but it's still a fact and facts must be respected. [2]

Because it was cold in Minnesota, even in summer, Prince stayed indoors and learned to play the guitars, keyboards, and drums that had been strewn about by his parents. You might say they were instrumental in his development. No, his parents were not Ozzie and Harriet Nelson. Let's shoot down that rumor at the outset.

At the age of fourteen months, Prince discovered that he was a musical genius, even though he could not pronounce the phrase for another year and a half. At the age of four, he became capable of rock stardom, but decided to hold off becoming one until puberty so he could understand sex and write erotic lyrics instead of songs about toys and baby blankets, which he considered uncommercial, though deeply satisfying. His first postpuberty song, written at the age of six, was titled, "Wow, So That's What This Thing Is For." He quickly followed that up with "I Gotta Find Me a Girl to Try This Thing Out On, Assuming I Turn Out to Be Heterosexual."

1. Okay, actually, as I write this, he's still alive but I really like this lead and anyway, someday he will be dead, so then it'll be accurate. Hold on to the book.

2. Though I have forgotten why.

Prince sometimes uses exotic costumes and props to trick audiences into believing that he is sexy.

To say that Prince was sexually precocious is, of course, an obvious statement, but that is no reason not to make it. The obvious is not always evident.

By the age of 21, Prince had made five albums, singing, writing the songs, playing all the instruments, tapping his own foot, building the recording equipment from scratch (which Minneapolis is full of), and carrying in coffee and doughnuts during breaks. He was not only a prodigy and a polymath but could also swivel his gaunt buttocks from side to side in a provocative manner, which won him many admirers.

A short, moist young man with puppylike eyes, an impudent pout, and a sparse growth of fuzz between his nostrils and upper lip, Prince was diagnosed by medical specialists as dangerously oversexed, thus ensuring that he would become a rock megastar. His candor often shocked the public, however. While most twentieth-century songwriters routinely employed the euphemism "love," Prince did not, preferring the more blatant Anglo-Saxon phrase, "doing that icky-sticky thing with our ninny-nogs."

He was prolific to the point of prolixity, churning out songs and albums even in his sleep. He affected an air of mystery, rarely giving interviews and sometimes hovering in midair, then vanishing in a puff of mauve smoke.

While still in his twenties, four of Prince's albums went platinum and one went aluminum. Touring with his band, the Princetonians, he would sometimes strip down to his Victoria's Secret black satin bikini underpants and climb into a brass bed onstage, where he would be flogged by Dominican monks until he cried, "Ouch!" or, on occasion, "Ee-yow!"

Yet despite being the world's biggest sexual exhibitionist until the advent of Paris Hilton, Prince was painfully shy offstage, not to mention weird. He often dashed behind potted plants when anyone approached him in public or at home, shouting, "I'm not here! You didn't see me!" He would sign autographs but only in disappearing ink.

There are many stories about Prince's eccentricities. On a concert tour in Europe, he was visited in his dressing room at London's Wembley Stadium by Prince Charles, who had brought his oldest son, Prince William, to the concert. Just as they arrived, another rock star, Freddie Mercury, dropped in. Introductions were made by the legendary B.B. King, who had opened for Prince. The conversation reportedly went as follows:

> *King:* "Prince, I'd like you to meet the Prince and his son, the Prince."
>
> *Prince:* "Thank you, King. Nice to meet you, Prince. You, too, Prince."
>
> *Prince:* "Prince, the honor is mine. I am a great Prince fan."
>
> *Prince:* "Thanks, Prince. How about you, Prince?"
>
> *Prince:* "Actually, Prince, I am unacquainted with your music. But I love your name."
>
> *King:* "Say, do you know Freddie? He is in Queen."
>
> *Prince:* "Really! I didn't even realize he knew the old bag."

In 1984, Prince vaulted to superstardom, despite a pulled hamstring on takeoff, with *Purple Rain*, which was a movie, an

JOCK ROCK

Little-Known Facts
about the
Sporting Side
of Rock and Roll

- Motley Crüe's Tommy Lee was a star outfielder for the Montreal Expos until he tested positive for every substance known to medical science.

- Boston Red Sox outfielder Johnny Damon isn't really a rock star; he just looks like one.

- Golf champion Tiger Woods recently released a soul album titled *Get Down and Bogey*. It featured guest appearances by Willie Nelson, Hootie and the Blowfish, and the Pips.

- Mick Jagger has an Olympic-size croquet court on the lawn of his chateau in the French town of Amboise and once played a game using the head of a local man who had offended him.

Continued on the following page's sidebar ☛

album, and a low-pressure zone that floated over the Midwest for a week. The film, about a brilliant, ambitious young man trying to succeed despite many obstacles, was widely regarded as biographical, though not about Prince, but rather Arnold Schwarzenegger. Prince made several other movies, including *Prince Valiant* and *The Prince of Tides*, but none had the lasting appeal of *Purple Rain*, which even today is regarded by aficionados as the best film ever made starring a short, annoying, half-naked sex maniac.

When Prince went through his name-changing phase, at one point insisting he be called the Artist Who in the Near Future Will Be Known as M. Reginald Putterby but You Can Call Me Putt, anxious fans huddled on street corners and in sex clubs, asking each other what was going on with their favorite entertainer. After a few minutes, they got bored and went home.

Prince continued releasing albums during the '90s, though his new name, the Guy Who Continues to Release Albums During the '90s, did nothing to allay the confusion surrounding his career. After a contract dispute with Warner Records, he had the word "Slave" tattooed on his face. This started a trend of celebrity tattooing, culminating with Dick Cheney sporting "Halliburton Rules" on his gluteus maximus.

By 1997, I had completely lost interest in Prince and thus am unable to continue the chapter. This is happening a lot lately. I hope this thing ends soon.

Chapter 42	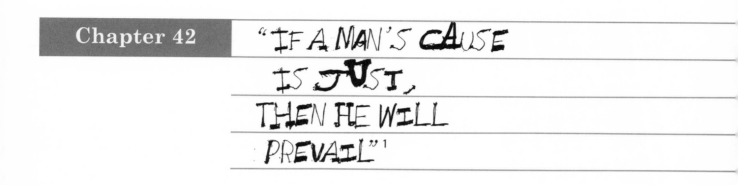

"IF A MAN'S CAUSE IS JUST, THEN HE WILL PREVAIL"[1]

On a clear night, at exactly 8:47 p.m. on Wednesday, January 28, 1985, with the barometer reading 73 degrees Fahrenheit, a cool wind blowing at sixteen miles per hour from the northeast, and a full moon overhead, forty-one music stars filed into the A&M recording studio located in a four-story brick Mission-style building located on 14373 La Cienega at the corner of Sunset Boulevard in Hollywood, California,[2] and began to sing a song written by Michael Jackson and Lionel Richie.

We are the world

We are big rock stars

We are the ones who make a brighter day

For those who aren't

Just by living

And lookin' really good

We let the little people know

How much we care

---

1. Attributed to O.J. Simpson.
2. Ever wonder where authors get all these amazing details? Mostly we make them up.

We are the world

We are the children

And God loves all the children

But not as much as He loves us

There are people

People dying in the world

But we're not them, we're stars

And we're all right

It was a historic moment, marred only when Ray Charles and Stevie Wonder got into one of their typical head-butting contests over who was the more legendary blind singer, but several other superstars quickly jumped in to break it up, suffering only superficial injuries. The point was that all these legends (among them Bob Dylan, Bruce Springsteen, Willie Nelson, Tina Turner, Paul Simon, Michael Jackson, Billy Joel, Kenny Rogers, Steve Perry, James Ingram, and Kim Carnes) had temporarily put aside their petty hatreds, envy, blood feuds, and lust for vengeance to work together for a noble cause.

Over the years, the main cause championed by rock stars has been the one expressed in that oft-shouted motto, "Sex, drugs, and rock and roll!" But there are always exceptions to everything and rock and roll is no exception to those exceptions. Rockers have sung and fought and killed for every cause from charity to world peace to protecting the environment to gaining the right to beat up the sleazy stalker/photographers who make their every waking moment a living hell.

There were those like Bob Geldof, the Irish rocker who started out as lead singer of the Boomtown Rats (a group known to every man, woman, and child in the British Isles and to no one anywhere else) and ended up the Mother Teresa of the music world. Nominated for a Nobel Peace Prize, named an honorary knight by Queen Elizabeth, and narrowly losing out to John Paul II as Pope, Geldof raised millions of dollars for feeding the poor and replacing their broken guitar strings.

There was U2, perhaps the only major band to ever have not one but *two* members with goofy names, namely Bono (pronounced, for no known reason, "bonno") and the Edge (pronounced "theedge"). Starting as a typical punk group with no one able to play, sing, or read, U2 rose to legend, if not institution, status through a mix of hard work, commitment, and speaking in tongues. Along the way they campaigned for political and social reform, often exhorting

Can you name every star in this photo? If so, there may be something seriously wrong with you.

audiences to stop wasting their money on stupid rock concerts and albums and instead go help the Third World. The Third World pleaded desperately for them to stay home.

Strangest of all for makers of rock and roll, U2 was religious, with three of its four members belonging to a bizarre cult known for worshiping an Aramaic-speaking Jewish carpenter who allegedly died more than two thousand years ago in a backwater of the Roman Empire. This was a harbinger of weirdness to come; the '80s and '90s would see an explosion of sacred rockers and holy rollers.

Christianity led the way, schisming up as usual into warring sects. Catholics tended to favor holy metal, giving rise to bands such as Vatykyn and Deep Papal, the latter famous for its number-one hit, "The Host Ain't Just Some Cracker." The evangelical punk band Jesus H. Fuckin' Christ charted in 1989 with its somewhat militant album *On Your Knees or Die!* and the country-oriented Baptist trio Oh for Christ's Sake, fronted by defrocked minister Halo, made a splash in 1993 with its double album, *Jesus Got Your Back.*

But Christian rock was just one woolly strand in the bulky red cable-knit sweater that was religious rock. Jews developed the popular electric-klezmer genre, whose best-known star was of course Dov Dingleman, the Reform Jewish blues belter from Boca Raton whose "Oy, Am I Down" and its follow-up "You Shouldn't Know from How Bad I'm Feelin'" were huge hits in 1997. The controversial Hasidic underground band Torah Boys made a stir the next year with the album *Go to Shul or Go to Hell* and the Jewish-agnostic group the Who Knows broke through to fame with its tantalizing soft rocker "Don't Ask."

Islamic rock made a promising start in the early '90s but was plagued with political problems. A big setback occurred in 1995 when the up-and-coming Iraqabilly band Dromedary, while on tour in Saudi Arabia, was beheaded by government security forces for blasphemy, beer drinking, and plagiarism. Still, there were notable breakthroughs as groups such as Electric Qatar, the Infidels, and Jihad achieved international success despite being branded terrorists by the U.S. government. Also, the banished but unbowed Kuwaiti rapper Little Allah Hallah Leujah, a protégé of Cat Stevens, scored with a whole string of hits including "Holy Shiite," "Sunni Days," and "I'd Like to Getcha on a Hip-Hop Hajj to Mecca."

Perhaps the most unusual religious rock genre was that begun by the ancient-Greek revival band Vestal Virgin, whose goal, it announced in 2001, was to singlehandedly bring back "that *really* old-time religion." Lead singer Terri Wimmel won a big following with her ballad, "That Wasn't Zeus, Sister," the heartbreaking saga of a woman seduced by a lying swan. But the band fell apart after it gave a concert at the Acropolis, causing a large crack in the 2,500-year-old temple, for which band members blamed each other. After that, much of the enthusiasm went out of Greco-Roman rock.

Cher, shown with an acolyte, during her religious phase, when she became an Aztec priestess and performed human sacrifices atop pyramids.

Chapter 43	TECH IT
	OR
	LEAVE IT

Throughout the history of rock and roll, there has always
existed a cluster of feckless fops (not that I'm biased or anything) who insisted that the music was for dancing, not listening. It was this effete, leg-obsessed cult that had brought down upon a cringing world such travails as disco, the twist, the mosh pit, and the mosh pendulum. But its most irritating invention was yet to come. Because these people lived in a technological age when everything was in Technicolor, they called that invention techno.

Technically, techno is computer-generated dance music, which means that no one fully understands how it is made except Bill Gates and his secretary. I shall attempt to explain it nonetheless. You would be disappointed if I did not. You have come to expect much from me. And rightfully so, for I have vowed that I will never disappoint you. But if I do, tough.

OK, what happens is a DJ (short for digital joker), utilizing a web-based, high-density splitter, feeds a 486 kHz audio stream into an integrated adjustable adapter affording analog playback with full-spectrum impedance. This process produces frequency resolution independent of sine-wave distortion or phase differential, all of which generates sound that is so loud it causes microscopic lacerations on the surface of the brain, enabling the listener to also receive music and commercials broadcast by very hip aliens on the planet Neptune.

And the dancing is sublime. Many of the dancers are in ecstasy. Others are on Ecstasy. In the '80s and early '90s, techno aficionados in London, Detroit, and San Francisco would gather at secret midnight conclaves known as raves. Often stoned on mild hallucinogenics such as prune juice, they would sacrifice a virgin or two over a roaring bonfire just to kick off the festivities. Then they would form a conga line and go snaking along through the darkness, shimmying to the pulsing, hypnotic techno beat. Arriving at a cliff, they would plummet into the abyss one by one until either the entire line had danced to its doom or the cops showed up, whichever came first.

Oddly enough, around 1998, the rave phenomenon began to fade away. The now-small techno community was puzzled over what was causing this reduction of the fan base.

Though most of the remaining techno DJs preferred to stay anonymous, due to modesty and fear of vengeful attack by enraged parents, a few finally began to step forward, remove their ear plugs, and seek the fame and wealth that every American is guaranteed in the U.S. Constitution.

The best known of these was the uni-appellated Moby, often called the Captain Ahab of Techno and sometimes just called Dick. An expert in all styles of techno, including ambient, trance, coprophagous, and house (a subgenre[1] that can only be played indoors), Moby is known for his clean living, abstaining from alcohol, drugs, meat, tobacco, and music.

A great multitasker, Moby has been known to perform concerts at which he prints out hard copies of his music at the same time he is playing it. He is amazingly versatile. At a stadium appearance in Akron, he was unfazed when his PC crashed. Borrowing an electric razor and a vacuum cleaner from audience members, he played his entire repertoire using only those two instruments and received a standing ovation plus the ears and tail of a bull that had been waiting in a pen for a rodeo scheduled the next day.

While no one knows what the future may hold for Moby, or that poor, earless, tailless bull, it does seem clear that with more and more of us humans being replaced every day by robotic machinery, techno is certain to be the music of tomorrow.

---

1. Like any respectable subgenre, house is divided into sub-subgenres. Among the more than 19,623 varieties of house are deep house, trance, progressive house, UK garage, trip-hop, poor house, circuit, out house, hiNrg, whore house, nu soul, mortgaged house, mad house, breakbeat, starter house, jungle, haunted house, Balearic, house of the rising sun, freestyle, house of lords, bleak house, monkey house, colonel house, letsplay house, omigod he's in the house, commonnamy house, and barbarawood house.

The eureka moment!
Scientists at Lunatech Labs
successfully test the
electronic synthelizer, which
will make possible both techno
music and a more accurate
measurement of blood alcohol.

Flaws, Errors, Peculiarities, Mistakes, Glitches, and Anomalies on Well-Known Recordings

☞ Studio air conditioners turned up on their highest setting are audible in the background as the Lovin' Spoonful sing "Summer in the City."

☞ A sound engineer on the Beatles' "My Bonnie Lies Over the Ocean" can be heard moaning, "I can't believe they're doing this crappy song. God, it's awful."

☞ When Metallica's 1983 album *Kill 'Em All* is played backwards, Dave Mustaine shouts, "They're trying to kick me out of this band, but that's okay; I will found Megadeth, where my mood swings, my outspokenness, and my excessive drug use will be better tolerated."

☞ Recording in an old studio plagued by leaky plumbing, Van Morrison audibly complains, "Oh, oh, the water," as he is doused from above on the song "And It Stoned Me."

☞ At the end of the Mamas and the Papas' 1966 song "I Saw Her Again," Mama Cass Elliot can be heard saying, "Mine's the cheeseburger with extra fries."

☞ During Silly Putty's 1983 recording of "Feets, Do Your Stuff," a fistfight occurred in the booth between sound engineer Bob Frocus and A&R man Arthur Cordry and then fire broke out in the studio when a backup singer's cigarette set a newspaper ablaze. The band continued playing throughout, even as firemen rushed into the studio and began breaking things and spraying water all over the place.

☞ On the last cut of its last album, *Insufficient Data*, the West Coast thrash band Various Artists can actually be heard breaking up. Listen for bassist Sammy Cromwell's scream of "I fuckin' quit" and the sound of his guitar being smashed over lead singer Mark Puttersbaugh's head.

☞ On G.G. Allin's last album, *The Murder Junkies Live at Attica*, Allin audibly strangles a corrections officer while the audience cheers.

Chapter 44 — HOLDING A GRUNGE AGAINST SOCIETY

The strange story of grunge is a classic illustration of the dangers of refusing to learn history. When a talented new generation of young musicians came along in the late '80s, rebelled against the rock establishment, and invented punk rock, they failed to realize that it had already been invented by the previous talented new generation. These poorly informed rebels didn't even get the name right, calling it grunge.

But at least grunge was the first trend to come out of Seattle—that is, unless you count the Boeing jumbo jet, which makes almost as much noise.

Another important contribution of the grungesters was to popularize the plaid flannel shirt. Previously worn only by lumberjacks and Scottish bagpipers (though tied around their waists and called a "kilt"), the PFS is a magnificent article of apparel: comfortable, warm, and snazzy-looking. It can be worn either with jeans in a casual setting or together with a blazer and gray or khaki trousers for slightly more formal occasions, given today's more relaxed standards. (I have a thing for plaid flannel shirts.)

The plaid flannel shirts were found mainly in garages, the venue of choice for Seattle bands. In the garage, your parents could not hear you play, thus averting familial bloodshed. As the guys in garages ground out their grunge, they vowed to each other that they would never "sell out" to the corrupt evil corporate-rock establishment, even if offered millions of dollars. Many kept the pledge and are still in the garage to this day, though middle-aged and quite hungry.

The flannelest and most grungiose band in Seattle's garagey world was Nirvana, a word that comes from a Buddhist slang expression meaning the ultimate beatitude that transcends suffering, karma, and samsara and is achieved through the extinction of desire and individual consciousness or, in the case of non-Buddhists, through drugs and alcohol. Nirvana is the band that took the electrifying message of Seattle grunge into the mainstream. That message was: *We're really pissed off but we don't know why.*

Take away the lyrics, however, and the subtext was more like: *ba da badaa daa dah dum.* It was an urgent, if imprecise, appeal.

Nirvana was composed of Kurt Cobain (real name: Curt Kobain), and two other guys whose names I can never remember, though I know one of them is really tall. Cobain was the product of a broken home; he tried to mend it but had only duct tape, which was not strong enough. After growing up listening to new wave and hardcore, whatever they were, he founded the band Fecal Matter, then became depressed when audiences kept shouting "You guys are shit!" He vowed that his next band would have a much better name. Even so, it turned out he was permanently depressed.

With its huge hit, "Smells Like Teen Spirit" (later to become the name of a best-selling cologne for cheerleaders), Nirvana celebrated the joys of anarchy and nihilism which, everyone but Republicans had to admit, were now the underlying principles of American life. In fact, the song was so successful that Nirvana had to leave its garage to wave at the millions of fans milling outside and thus immediately was accused of selling out. Painful and confusing as this experience was, it led to the band's next hugely selling album, *We Just Went Out for a Smoke, That's All.*

Nirvana finally solved its selling-out problem by forming an offshoot band composed of friends and relatives. The members of this group, Pearl Jam, were not quite so pure and therefore were permitted to play stadiums and become enormously rich.

As fine a guitarist and songwriter as he was, Kurt Cobain was even more talented as a suicide. After two preliminary attempts, which the critics termed promising though uneven, he finally broke through in 1994 when his first effort at playing a shotgun proved spectacularly successful. Fans and critics alike hailed his act and unanimously voted him into the Rock Pantheon of Legendary Icons, built last week in Chillicothe, Ohio.

An entire generation now regards Nirvana as its version of the Beatles. They are of course hopelessly mistaken, but I would not recommend you tell them so.

As acclaim grew for Nirvana and its imitators, the remaining practitioners of grungistic music became terribly embarrassed by their success, which was diluting their rage and alienation from society. In response, they issued a press release stating that grunge had been an invention of the media, there was no such thing, and that the stuff they were playing was not grunge or punk or hair metal or industrial rock but "alternative." Alternative rock, they maintained, was preferable to and much cooler than the "mainstream" music being put out by the evil and corrupt rock establishment.

Upon hearing this, the E&CRE immediately began producing and marketing alternative rock, especially through its enforcement arm, MTV. At that point, it became very difficult to tell what alternative music was the alternative to.

Fortunately, there was always the option to simply not care.

Tempestuous, unpredictable Courtney Love tells Pizza Hut that if her order takes more than ten minutes to arrive or contains anchovies, she will shoot the delivery boy.

The Five Best **Rock Movies** of the Last 25 Years

☞ **The Last Polka** *(1982)* ★★★★

Legendary director Ingmar Bergman came out of an assisted-living facility to film Abba's retirement tour of Scandinavia and the Baltic states. But this is more than just another concert film; Bergman's probing, penetrating camera reveals the shocking hostilities, jealousies, and reproach festering just beneath the sunny façade of Abba's mindless disco harmonies. The final scene, in which an agonized Björn Ulvaeus admits to Agnetha "Anna" Fältskog that he is a secret heavy-metal fan, is so shattering that many moviegoers retched in despair.

☞ **The Divine Tragedy** *(1989)* ★★★★

Blondie, Divine, and David Carradine played themselves in this John Waters remake of Dante's masterpiece in which a washed-up rock star (John Travolta) who has suffered a fatal drug overdose can only be released from an eternity of torment in Hell if, in one day on earth, he can find three people who still own one of his albums. (Look for Bob Dylan's intriguing cameo as a sadistic but unintelligible demon.)

☞ **A Horse with No Name** *(1991)* ★★★★

Michael Cimino's ill-fated attempt to revive the rock-western genre tanked at the box office but became a cult favorite. Bruce Willis and Willie Nelson played the Lone Ranger and Tonto, respectively, and Linda Ronstadt made for an unexpectedly tender Calamity Jane. Van Halen's soundtrack album sold dozens of copies.

☞ **The Grunge Who Stole Christmas** *(2000)* ★★★★

This uplifting Bob Zemeckis comedy stars Will Ferrell, Jack Black, and Meat Loaf as three elves assigned to steal the spirit of Christmas back from an evil wizard (Marilyn Manson) who has gained control of all the world's radio stations and decreed that no Christmas music may be played ever again, especially "The Little Drummer Boy," which makes him want to blow his brains out. (Randy Newman penned the score.)

☞ **The Dissin' Dozen** *(2001)* ★★★★

Twelve gangsta rappers from the hood are recruited to form a WWII commando unit for a secret mission to drive Hitler into a fatal apoplectic fit by transmitting degenerate hip-hop over the PA system of his Berlin bunker. P. Diddy stars as Mean Mutha, the tough kid with a chip on his shoulder and a helmet always worn backwards. Ice-T plays his no-nonsense commanding officer, General Patton, and Cuba Gooding Jr. is the sensitive poet/sniper who's afraid he doesn't fit in.

Chapter 45	HOW AMERICA GOT FUNKED UP

Some thought funk was junk. Others called it bunk. A few confused it with punk. But many believed it showed spunk. I could go on like this a lot longer but I'm guessing you can't take much more.

In 1982, funk replaced soul. Something had to. Every ten years, another thing comes along. Black, white, or gray, we Americans must have novelty or we shrivel and die. You know that, right? Then why are you looking at me that way?

The origins of funk are mysterious. We do know that James Brown had something or other to do with it but no one has been brave enough to ask him exactly what. The trouble is that the word sounds nasty. Whenever you hear "funk" or "funky," the mental image you summon up always involves an article of underwear that has recently gone through a disgraceful experience.

In fact, no one was allowed to utter the word in polite society or even the upper reaches of rude society until 1967 when Dyke and the Blazers (a name already teetering on the edge of unacceptability) broke through with their AM radio hit, "Funky Broadway." After that, other funk groups emerged from hiding with such follow-ups as "Funky Park Avenue," "Funky Elm Street," "Funky New York State Thruway," and "Funky Parking Lot Outside the Funky A&P Supermarket."

In any serious discussion of funk, however, ultimately one name predominates: George Clinton. Okay, I guess that's actually two names. Sorry. Anyway, he is Mr. Funk, the Funkmeister, the Knight of the Graceful Funkitude, Doctor Funkenstein's Monster, the Grand Mufti of Funkadelphia, and the Frankly Funkicidal Funkster of Funkdom. Yes, George Clinton is to funk what Paris Hilton is to underwear that has recently gone through a disgraceful experience.

It was in the mid-'50s, while still working as an assistant hair puller in a New Jersey barbershop, that Clinton began presiding over a loose and ever-evolving assortment of musicians known by various names, the least ridiculous of which were Parliament and Funkadelic. These musicians would sit around at home resting until the phone rang and the voice of George Clinton was heard, saying: "Get the funk down here, motherfunker." Then they would rush over to George's place to see what that funking guy was funking up this time.

Usually it was something like George in a long blond wig jumping out of a coffin while the band wore diapers, smoked marijuana, and simulated sex acts while playing "Tear the Roof Off the Sucker" or "Atomic Dog" or "Maggot Brain" or tunes from the albums *Funkentelechy vs. the Placebo Syndrome* or *The Electric Spanking of War Babies* or *Hey Man …Smell My Finger*. You know, just the usual, bland, commercial-radio stuff.

This went on for about forty years, with George and the various offshoots, hybrids, spinoffs, and whirligigs of his tribe going from cult objects to hitmakers to inspirers of mainstream funk and hip-hop to subjects of numerous medical textbooks on deviant behavior.

George Clinton.

(Hey, they can't all be hilarious.)

Other funk facilitators such as Kool and the Gang and Earth, Wind, and Fire came and went as the world passed through its usual cycles of war, peace, recession, and giggling regression to infancy. But in the funkocracy, only Clinton was able to turn his funkular vision into a religion that ministered to believers and crusaded against false idols who, in the view of Cardinal Funkelieu (George again), dared to fake the funk.

In 1998, the other F-word finally had the honor of making the dictionary. Well, just one dictionary, actually. Funk and Wagnall's.

Funk ruled the black charts through the '80s and into the '90s until one day rap came hip-hopping along and suddenly, like its beloved ancestors, soul, rhythm and blues, Motown, and Negro spirituals, funk was defunkt. But George Clinton's influence would live on in the music of many hip-hop, jazz, and rock musicians; the work of the Juilliard String Quartet; and the policies of the International Monetary Fund, which so clearly owe much to his scatological imagery and dismal ecstasy.

As George had thundered unto his acolytes so many times, "Free your mind and your ass will follow." Now, at long last, his ass was free to follow any mind it chose. And vice versa.

Places Where
Rock and Roll Has
Never
Really Been
Understood

1. Saudi Arabia
2. Tibet
3. France
4. Utah
5. North Korea
6. Buckingham Palace
7. The Vatican
8. Jerry Falwell's house
9. PBS
10. Bob Jones University

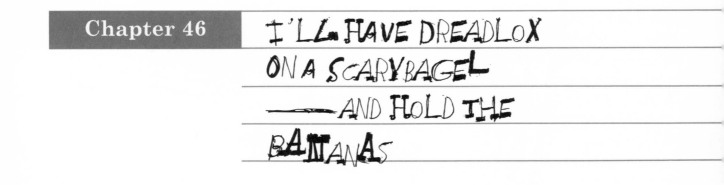

Chapter 46

I'LL HAVE DREADLOX ON A SCARY BAGEL — AND HOLD THE BANANAS

Reggae originated in Jamaica, which is a beautiful tropical paradise for everyone except the people who have to live there. For them it's a Third-World hellhole. But on the upside, one with lots of music and drugs.

In the old days Jamaican music was known as calypso. Calypso was a gentle style of folk music with a syncopated beat and simple lyrics that were charming and also slightly nauseating. Most of the tunes were about either making love under a banana tree or being bitten by a deadly tarantula while making love under a banana tree. Often cowbells, bongos, steel drums, and other forms of comic percussion were involved.

Since Jamaica was a small place, calypso could only have one star at a time. Usually it was Harry Belafonte. When he finally left for a career in U.S. show biz, the Jamaicans sat around depressed until rock and roll reached the Caribbean. Then they combined the two and came up with reggae, a Rastafarian word having two meanings, "louder" and "angrier."

The Rastafarians are members of a Jamaican religious cult that worships a god called Ganja. In an effort to gain converts, Rastafarian preachers frequently stand on street corners asking passersby, "Hey, mon, want some Ganja?"

You can always tell a Rastaman by his dreadlocks and his habit of calling everyone "mon," which in the rich patois of the islands, means "asshole." The patois is very colorful and expressive. For instance, if a Rasta should say to you, "Dem bandulus fi bong belly pickney, fe see we boonoonoonous a likkle," this means, "Hey, mon, want some Ganja?"

In the '60s, reggae burst into international renown through the music of Bob Marley and his group the Wailers, and also a movie titled *The Harder They Come*. Starring Jimmy Cliff, the film told the story of a young man born and raised in the country-side who comes to the slums of Kingston, the capital, to be hassled by the police so he will have something to sing about.

All reggae stars are born and raised in the countryside and come to the slums of Kingston, the capital, to be hassled by the police so they will have something to sing about. The police are only too happy to cooperate because they know the island's economy depends on exporting reggae records. Also, they are sadistic brutes.

Bob Marley was no exception to the rule. Born and raised in the countryside, Marley came to the slums of Kingston, the capital, to be hassled by the police so he would have something to sing about. But because he had immense talent, he was hassled even more than the other reggae stars. The Jamaican police can always spot a comer.

The hassle experience inspired one of Marley's biggest hits, "I Shot the Sheriff." In this song, the narrator, a man called "I," admits to having shot the sheriff, though claiming it was self-defense. And then he famously sings, "But I didn't shoot no deputy," adding, just in case you don't believe him, "Oh no."

The question that has always raged within top reggae circles is: "Then who did shoot the deputy?" Opinions vary. Some think it was bad, bad Leroy Brown. After all, he was the baddest man in town.

Reggae star Bunny Wailer grows disconsolate as he realizes that his dreadlocks have taken on a life of their own and are trying to crawl off his head.

Deadly Bananas

Microsoft Word has a fabulous tool for writers called AutoSummarize. This ingenious device can take a piece of writing and extract the key sentences to form a summary containing all the important points with no excess verbiage. Here, for the benefit of busy executives who don't have the time to read all of Chapter 46, is the AutoSummarize version:

Most of the tunes were about either making love under a banana tree or finding a deadly tarantula while picking bananas off the banana tree. The Rastafarians are members of a Jamaican religious cult that worships a god called Ganja. In the '60s, reggae burst into international renown through the music of Bob Marley and his group the Wailers and also a movie titled *The Harder They Come*, starring Jimmy Cliff.

The police are only too happy to cooperate because they know the island's economy depends on exporting reggae records. Bob Marley was no exception to the rule. Born and raised in the countryside, Marley came at an early age to the slums of Kingston, the capital, and was hassled by the police. This experience inspired one of his biggest hits, "I Shot the Sheriff." The question that has always raged within reggae circles is: "Then who did shoot the deputy?" Not from shooting, like most reggae stars, but cancer. There have been other reggae stars but they do not interest us.

Others say it was Frankie, of Frankie and Johnny fame, who had a reputation for shooting men who had done her wrong. Still others insist that Mack the Knife was back in town, pearly teeth, scarlet billows, and all. Personally, I've always suspected Eric Clapton, but I can't prove anything.

It's a fact that the song never took off until the English blues-guitar virtuoso covered it in 1974. Though Clapton looked guilty as hell, his alibi—that at the time of the shooting he was with Layla and her sister, Sally, trying to get Sally to lay down—held up under intense interrogation, so the cops let him walk. But don't worry; I'm keeping an eye on Clapton. This thing isn't over yet, believe me.

Musicologically speaking (a kind of speaking we usually avoid here but okay, just this once), reggae has the best backbeat in all of rock, an infectious rhythm that (caution: genuine simulated Jamaican patois follows) gots dem a go jump an shake de leg. Unfortunately, the frontbeat seldom measures up.

But getting back to Bob Marley, the basic story is he became a big international show-biz star and then he died. Not from shooting, like most reggae stars, but cancer. Very sad, but at least he made legend status and today is firmly ensconced in the Reggae Hall of Fame in Binghamton, New York. Bob's son, Ziggy Marley, has carried on the family tradition despite his silly name, recording with his band, the Melody Makers. There are other reggae stars, of course, and someday, when all the fuss dies down, you and I may sit back with a couple of beers and have a long chat about them.

Chapter 47	BEST

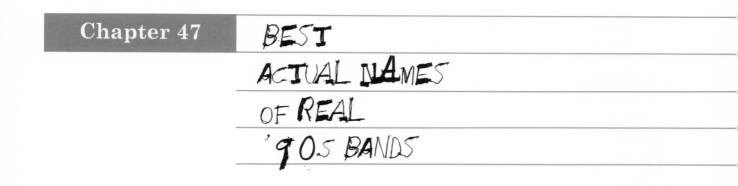

BEST
ACTUAL NAMES
OF REAL
'90s BANDS

The decade of the '90s was a rotten time for music but it was by far the greatest era for band names. Why this is, we do not know. Perhaps the bands used up all their creative energy in the naming phase. When coming up with names, the '90s bands[1] were totally unafraid to exploit death, sex, insanity, religion, race, puns, insects, deformity, non sequiturs, references too obscure for anyone to understand, and other subjects once considered taboo in pop culture. Or maybe they were just sicker than musicians of earlier times. Of all the many-splendored band names below, my favorite is The The. But that's just me. Every one of them is real, by the way. Except for one, which I have made up just so we can have a contest. Won't that be fun! The prize? The first reader who sends in the correct answer will be allowed to take the author out to dinner. (For those of you who don't want to enter the contest but just want to know the answer, it may be found on the bottom of page 202. I know that no one will look it up and then enter the contest because we're on the honor system here and my kind of reader would never cheat.)

2 Foot Flame	Armageddon Dildos	Barenaked Ladies
3rd Bass	Arrested Development	Bassholes
10,000 Maniacs	Babe the Blue Ox	Beatnik Filmstars
Aints	Bad Brains	Belly
Amorphous Androgynous	Bad Religion	Best Kissers in the World

---

1. To be honest, some of these groups started in the '80s and were still around in the '90s. Please don't get mad. It's only a book.

Perry Farrell, former lead singer with Jane's Addiction and Porno for Pyros, still has the fashion flair that made him one of the best-dressed and most urbane entertainers of the nineties.

Better Than Ezra
Biff Bang Pow!
Bizarr Sex Trio
Blohole
Bloodloss
Boo Radleys
Boredoms
Brotherhood of Lizards
Butt Trumpet
Carmaig de Forest's Death Groove Love Party
Carter the Unstoppable Sex Machine
Christian Death
Circle Jerks
Cleaners from Venus
Coffin Break
Cop Shoot Cop
Cowboy Junkies
Cramps
Crash Test Dummies
Cud
Cycomotogoat
Dancing French Liberals of '48
Dashboard Saviors
Dead Can Dance
Dead Milkmen
Dead Presidents
Dead Voices on Air

Dentists
Deep Blue Something
Disposable Heroes of Hiphoprisy
D.O.A.
Drink Me
Drive Like Jehu
Drywall
Dylans
Earwig
East River Pipe
Eat
Echobelly
E. Coli
Eggs
Egomaniacs
Eight or Nine Feet
Einstürzende Neubauten [2]
Elastic Purejoy
Elvis Brothers
Emergency Broadcast Network
Everything But the Girl
Failure
Fakes
Fig Dish
Fitz of Depression
Flop
Fly Ashtray
Flying Saucer Attack

2. Translated from German, the phrase means "Collapsing New Buildings."

Foo Fighters

For Squirrels

Friggs

Geggy Tah

Glands of External Secretion

Goats

Gobblehoof

God

Guild of Temporal
Adventurers

Halo Benders

Handsome Family

Henrietta Collins and the
Wifebeating Childhaters

High Risk Group

Jane's Addiction

Kathleen Turner Overdrive

Kicking Giant

Kill Sybil

Killer Shrews

King Kong

Kitchens of Distinction

Laughing Hyenas

Lay Quiet Awhile

Lazy Cowgirls

Lee Harvey Oswald Band

Letters to Cleo

Life, Sex & Death

Love Interest

Machines of Loving Grace

Maids of Gravity

Manic Street Preachers

MC 900 Ft. Jesus

Meathook Seed

Meat Puppets

Melvins

Menster Phip and the
Phipsters

Molly Half Head

Monks of Doom

Moonpools and Caterpillars

Motherhead Bug

Mouse on Mars

Moxy Früvous

Mummies

Mule

My Dad Is Dead

My Bloody Valentine

My Life with the Thrill Kill
Kult

My Head

Napalm Death

Naughty by Nature

Ned's Atomic Dustbin

Neurotic Outsiders

New Fast Automatic
Daffodils

New Wet Kojak

Noel Coward's Ghost

Noise Addict

Nosferatu

Nothing Painted Blue

No Use for a Name

Oblivious

Olympic Death Squad

Petty and Twisted

pHoaming Edison

Pigface

Pop Art Toasters

Pop Will Eat Itself

Porno for Pyros

Premature Ejaculation

Presidents of the United
States of America

Rage Against the Machine

Rake's Progress

Rest in Pieces

Revolting Cocks

Robert Fripp and the League
of Crafty Guitarists

Rocket from the Crypt

Rollerskate Skinny

Rosetta Stone

Rump

Screeching Weasel

Shadowy Men on a Shadowy
Planet

Shudder to Think

Silver Jews

Simple Minds

Sludgeworth

Smashing Pumpkins

Smoking Popes

Sneetches

Spin Doctors

Sordid Humor

Soul Coughing

Southern Culture on the Skids

Squirrel Nut Zippers

Stanford Prison Experiment

Stigmata a Go Go

Stinky Puffs

Straitjacket Fits

Strapping Fieldhands

Suddenly, Tammy!

Suicidal Tendencies

Surgery

Swingin' Neckbreakers

Tall Dwarfs

Television Personalities

Temple of the Dog

Texas Instruments

The The

These Animal Men

They Might Be Giants

Thinking Fellers Union Local
282

This Mortal Coil

Thomas Jefferson Slave
Apartments

Three Day Stubble

Throw That Beat in the
Garbagecan!

Thrown Ups

Tightie Whities

Toad the Wet Sprocket

Toiling Midgets

Too Much Joy

Tragically Hip

Trash Can Sinatras

Treat Her Right

Trenchmouth

Tumor Circus

Type O Negative

Unsane

Vacant Lot

Vehicle Flips

Voluptuous Horror of Karen
Black

Vowel Movement

Vulgar Boatmen

When People Were Shorter
and Lived Near the Water

World of Skin

You and What Army

Chapter 48

RAP
RAP...
WHO'S THERE?

To best relate the tumultuous and ear-splitting history of rap, aka hip-hop, your fatigable but still game author conducted an exclusive interview with the iconic figure whose career spans the gamut of the genre, the legendary rapper, producer, actor, men's-hat designer, and trainer of champion pit bulls, Big Krocka S.

Tell us how you helped start the hip-hop revolution.

What you mean, *helped*, muthafucka? Yo, check it out. Y'all Google "hip-hop" plus "start of," what you get? 'Bout nine badillion hits all sayin' "Big Krocka S, he the man!"

We stand corrected. Tell us about the early days of rap.

How it all started was, back in the day, me and my crew we was in Bed Stuy, gettin' paid, you know what I'm sayin'?

Committing crimes?

Ay yo, thuggin'. In the hood, a man got to do what a man got to do. The life it be 'bout survivin', not jivin'.

But didn't you actually grow up in Huntington, Long Island, and graduate from Yale?

What you lookin' fo', bitch, somebody to pop a cap in yo' ass? I be street, dawg. I keepin' it real. Okay, lissen up, I was just chillin' in New Haven so's I could pick up a sheepskin

Big Krocka S (top row, right) and his crew are sworn in during a 2001 trial involving the death of a rival rapper. All six were cleared after Big testified that he was in Stockholm receiving the Nobel Peace Prize at the time of the accidental stabbing.

but summatimes I'm gettin' down with the bloods in the hood. The Stuy, baby! I jumped into the game befo' the game was the game. Me and my posse, we intro'd a new martial-art form. Break-neckin', I called it.

Break-neckin'?

Yeah. Tha's slang fo' breakin' somebody's neck. See, any mutha-fucka try to fuck me up, I'ma flip upside down, spin 'round on top my head—watchin' alla that spinnin' an' flippin' goin' dizzy 'em up—and then I'ma kick 'em in the face. One time we was beefin' with some wack niggaz and I had my boom box, it blastin' James Brown. Shee-it, we kick they ass so hard a whole crowda niggaz be standin' 'round givin' us props. Sendin' us mad love. They like, "Yo! Keep it crackin'!" So we do. And that's how break-neckin' become break-dancin'.

I never knew that. That's amazing.

Word. After that, we be bustin' some moves in the clubs, me and my b-boys and fly girls. But then one time I hadda fly outta a second-floor window cuz some dumb-ass nigga show up in his crib when I be bonin' his ho. So's I couldn't bust it no mo' on the flo' cuz I busted my fuckin' leg.

Is that when you turned to rapping?

Yeah, one a my homeys, he the DJ at Club Bootylicious up in Harlem, he ax me, "Yo, why don' you git up an' sing?" I'm like, "Cuz I cant fuckin' carry a fuckin' tune, tha's why." So he's like, "OK, whodi, just rap while I'm DJin'." Back in the day, "rap" just meant "talk," you know what I'm sayin? Just like step up and bullshit. So I start spittin' and the niggaz, they all like, "Shee-it, you the man!" Next thing you know, every nigga in the hood who want to be a playa be bitin' my lines and it wasn't long 'fore some caucasiaz was, too. Alls of a sudden these wack suckas that can't sing, can't move, can't do shit, they up there rappin' and thinkin' they the bomb.

But you couldn't sing, dance, or play an instrument either, right?

C'mon, man. I ain't got to. I be a genius.

But wasn't it Grandmaster Flash who invented modern DJing when, in the mid-'70s, he started jumping the needle around on his turntables while switching channels on a mixer?

Fuck, no! That was me done that, fool. Sometimes I was the DJ and the MC both. Flash, Run-DMC, Dre, all them niggaz, they all bit that shit offa me. Okay? You feelin' what I'm layin' down, muthafucka?

Fabulous Factoids

- Lil' Kim was called Big' Kim until she lost 342 pounds on the Atkins Diet.
- Bob Dylan's "Subterranean Homesick Blues," recorded in the early '60s, was actually the first rap song.
- Tupac Shakur, the idol of every young rapper and high-school athlete, started out as a singing, roller-skating carhop waiter at an L.A. hamburger joint.
- The short Detroit MC Rappelstiltskin is believed to be the world's only dwarf rapper.
- Not one single thing in this entire book is true. It is a gigantic pack of lies from beginning to end.
- Even that was a lie. Three or four things are true.
- Chinese President Hu Jintao loves to take out a boom box and play hip-hop at meetings of his Cabinet, sometimes making everyone get up and dance.

Complaint noted. What else did you invent?

Two of my most ass-kickin' concepts was D-librit mispellyn an' comin' off like a dumb-ass illiterate. Dawg, I ain't gotta talk like this; I copped a master's in sociology from fuckin' Princeton! But you gotta be street!

In that case, could you perhaps try to be less, um, vivid, for the rest of this interview? Some of my more sensitive readers may be offended by your language.

Well, how's 'bout I talk Ass-Tricks?

Ass-Tricks?

Yeah, tha's some sh*t I invented so's I could be quoted in the f**ckin' mainstream media. Never got credit for that, neither. Another one o' mine was cappin' muthaf***az that dissed me. Musta put at least a dozen m*thaz in they boxes fo' sho'. 'Course I got capped nine times myself. But I be hard. Can't keep me down nohow.

Can you tell us anything about the violence that claimed the lives of Tupac Shakur and other top rap stars?

Shee-*t, yeah. Fact I was chillin' with Notorious B.I.G. when he got gatted. It was a accident. Biggie got in front of my Glock when I was bustin' slugs at some mothaf***a what dissed me. Far as 'Pac, I think it was me capped his a*s, too, but I was suckin' on the pipe at the time so it be tough to tell.

The crack pipe?

Crack, smack, weed, all that dope dope. Now I be more 'bout takin' care o' business, but back in the day, I din' know who the f**k I was bustin' slugs at half the time an' din' care. Just bang here and bang there an' f**k all. Them days, it was nothin' but partyin' and gangsta s**t. An' man, it be boo-yaa! Sometimes I be missin' it, word is bond.

But isn't that type of wanton, lawless behavior completely immoral?

Okay, what you said right there? Tha's racist. Y'all be axin' Bush that s**t when he beef with one a them Middle East hoods? No way. You be wavin' flags an' all that red-white-an' blue bulls**t. But I pull the 'zact same s**t, you be dissin' me.

But by bragging about shooting people, aren't you setting a bad example for the younger generation?

Ay yo, b***h. It ain't braggin' on it if you really done it. Anyways, I be shinin' on lots of young muthaf***az. I be mentorin' they a*s.

Oh? Whom have you mentored?

How 'bout Eminem for one muthaf***a? Couple years ago, Em he stuck for a track on this new joint he gonna drop. So I tell him 'bout how this one time some h* dissed me so's I tie her up and stash her in the trunk o' my whip. An' he's like, "Yo, dude! That's so def!" An' I'm like, "S**t, dawg, nobody be sayin' 'def' no mo'; Tha's f**ked up." So he's like, "Oh, I meant 'phat.' " "F**kin' sh*t f*ck, dawg, tha's even worser!" So then he be all like,"Oh, shi*, sorry, sorry, sorry. Please don't tell nobody I said that, OK?" Cuz he be fu*kin' insecure, you know what I'm sayin'? Cuz he not really no brutha, he only just spit like one.

Not to get technical but actually, you're not African-American either, are you?

Say what? You gone psycho? You tryin' to punk me, m********a? You wanna war?

No, I was merely inquiring...

Nobody do me like that, *******! Nobody! You in hella trouble now.

 (At this point, Big Krocka S pulled a large gun from under his large sweatshirt and began firing in the air. Under the circumstances, your author felt it advisable to bring the interview to a close.)

Goodbye.

Bounce the f**k outta my crib, mut***ucka, or I'ma wax yo' as*.

Nice to meet you.

Yeah, yeah, sure. Ay yo, when's this dumb-*ss book comin' out? Y'all send me a copy, hear?

*Sure. When **** freezes o***.*

Chapter 49	ROCK
	AROUND
	THE
	EPOCH

And so now the human race races full speed into the murky depths of the twenty-first century, heedless as always of the consequences. With the growing threats from terrorism, global warming, nuclear proliferation, and the terrifying upsurge of stupidity, it is clear that our species and our planet can survive, at most, another decade. But that is not important. The crucial issue we must consider is: whither rock and roll?

In other words, will rock and roll wither when we get thither? Or will it wax, and if it does wax, will it take its shoes off to avoid marring the finish?

To some extent, we can predict the future by carefully studying the past, the present, and the subjunctive. We can do this by borrowing the techniques of the great futurologists, such prescient prognosticators as Nostradamus, Jeanne Dixon, the Amazing Kreskin, and Felicia Dworsky, who lives in the apartment above mine and can always sense when I am about to sleep for that is when she chooses to vacuum.[1]

Yea, I have done the homework and now I see taking shape before my astonished eyes the future of rock and roll. Oh my, is it ever weird. Things will happen, many things, things that cannot be stopped or understood, not even by the Christian Right, and these are only some of them:

---

1. One thing we can predict with utter certainty is that there will be no more of these annoying footnotes in the future of this book.

- Nude rock and roll becomes a huge trend in France until the U.S. threatens to invade.

- Etc., the first tribute band to imitate a tribute band, rises to the top of the charts with its versions of songs by Generic, the band dedicated to the works of Genesis.

- After giving up show biz to become a nun and spending eight years cloistered and silent in a Romanian convent repeating Mendel's genetic experiments with peas, Britney Spears makes a triumphant comeback and is hailed by critics for what they call "The New Seriosity." Before 90,000 fans at the Rose Bowl, she stands in the spotlight alone with an acoustic guitar and unveils a brilliant array of songs she has written displaying a profound new social and political vision that point the way to a radical transformation of society. As one, the audience rises to its feet and cries, "Take off your clothes, bitch!"

- President Jeb Bush (who succeeds his brother as President in 2008 after the Democrats lose the liberal vote) signs a bill prohibiting rock and roll. Rock and rollers are rounded up and sent to concentration camps. But a year later, the Supreme Court declares the law unconstitutional with Chief Justice Clarence Thomas writing for the majority, "Yes, rock and roll is immoral, but the founding fathers would have dug it, and besides, Janet Jackson is really hot!"

- Jay-Z astounds the hip-hop world with his album *Whassup, Putz?* in which, on every track, he raps in a Yiddish accent. He is whisked off to a private facility and given medications which restore his linguistic abilities to their normal state.

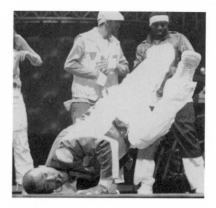

Attempting a tricky dance move on the Justin Timberlake/Christina Aguilera World Tour 2003, Justin got his right ear stuck in a small hole in the stage in Clearwater, Florida, and had to be rescued by emergency workers.

Given to impulsive decisions, Britney Spears was briefly married to this dolphin in 2002. The two are still good friends.

Answer to the Contest in Chapter 47:
Tightie Whities

- ☛ Mick Jagger falls and breaks a hip while singing "Street Fighting Man" at a concert in Las Vegas. Four months later, the Stones resume their concert tour with Mick back in good health, though using a walker.
- ☛ Kylie Minogue announces that henceforth the last two letters of her last name will no longer be silent and the stress will be placed on the first syllable.
- ☛ P. Diddy announces that he is changing his name to D. Piddy.
- ☛ The first a cappella rap album, by the multi-ethnic thrash-rap/crunk group Ga-Ga-a-Go-Go, sets the hip-hop world on its ear, causing dozens of broken eardrums. *Vibe* magazine christens the new form doohop and it sweeps across the face of the earth like some humongous musical tsunami.

Just from this summary alone, we can see that the revolution in music in the twenty-first century will be so tumultuous it will make the twentieth century seem like the nineteenth century. Fortunately, I'll be dead for most of it, but you may not have that option, so I suggest you begin your emergency preparations immediately.

Okay, that's it. I've covered the entire history of rock and roll and I'm exhausted. This book is finished, so quit reading and go back to your tenuous life. I know, we've had a few laughs together, we've bonded, but face it, it's over. I've done all I can to help you. Go home and leave me alone.

Oh, you are home? Sorry.

About the Author

Lewis Grossberger, recently ranked America's 126th funniest humorist by the American Academy of Rank Humorists, has written a whole bunch of stuff that has appeared in various places and probably won many prestigious writing awards that got lost in the mail or something. Born in Tahiti, the illegitimate son of Prince Philip of England and a half-wild Gypsy girl, he attended the Sorbonne, but was expelled for failing French. Before becoming a writer, he worked as a stevedore, a muleskinner, a pirate, and other colorful jobs that you aren't man enough to handle. He lives in New York City with his furniture and appliances. For career reasons, his wife, the actress Salma Hayek, refuses to acknowledge their relationship in public.

What Are You Laughing At?

If there's one thing we're serious about at Emmis Humor, it's funny business. On our list is the smart, smarting, occasionally smart-aleck, and even the if-you're-so-smart-why-aren't-you-rich?

We're aiming to publish books that bristle within the confines of a "humor section," books that politely refuse to be called bathroom reading, books you may have to explain to your ex. Emmis Humor means books with insight into human foibles with subjects ranging from politics to poetry, books with integrity, vision, and sticker fun. Yes, each volume comes with a sheet of stamps created just for that book.

Now that you're the proud owner of Lewis Grossberger's *Turn That Down*, check out Francis Heaney's *Holy Tango of Literature*, a dazzling, dizzying collection of parodies in which the author creates poems and plays inspired by anagrams of the names of great figures in the literary canon.

Also not to be missed: *Richard's Poor Almanac: Twelve Months of Misinformation in Handy Cartoon Form* by Richard Thompson (who, by the way, also illustrated *Holy Tango*). *Richard's Poor Almanac* is a year's compendium of weathered wisdom, gathered from seven years of his work in *The Washington Post*.

And, finally, for anyone who has ever cursed a squirrel, lawnmower, or neighbor, look forward to a rather deceptive yarn that purports to be the collected horticultural columns of one overly opinionated Mertensia Corydalis. Bonnie Thomas Abbott's book, *Radical Prunings: Officious Advice from the Contessa of Compost,* does to gardening what John Lanchester did for cooking in *A Debt to Pleasure*, or what Adam and Eve did for innocence in the Garden of Eden.

There's plenty more on the horizon. You'll want to collect 'em all.

Michael J. Rosen, series editor

An insubordinate Subdivision of Emmis Books

What are YOU laughing at?

emmis humor

emmis humor

The Old Firehouse
1700 Madison Road
Cincinnati, OH 45206

www.emmis.com/humor

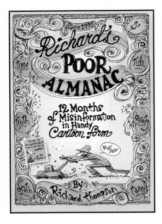

$14.95 Paperback
ISBN 1-57860-184-3

RICHARD'S POOR ALMANAC

by Richard Thompson

Four seasons of helpful, not so helpful, and just plain heretical advice…in case there's anyone out there who'd care to listen.

> *"If Benjamin Franklin were still alive, he would be wildly impressed by this book's cleverness, its irreverence, its exuberance, and the gentle genius that puts Richard Thompson among America's greatest living cartoonists. Then he would sue for copyright infringement. Ben was pretty shrewd and hostile for a Quaker."* —**Gene Weingarten** *The Washington Post*

$12.99 Paperback
ISBN 1-57860-159-2

HOLY TANGO OF LITERATURE

by Francis Heaney

What if poets and playwrights wrote works whose titles were anagrams of their names? This is the seldom-asked question Heaney answers here. English majors everywhere are dazzled:

> *"…a gob-smacking genius!"* —**David Rakoff**
>
> *"A very funny and possibly classic anthology."* —**Mark O'Donnell**
>
> *"…exquisite writing skills and considerable wit are utterly squandered in this trivial literary pastiche—which is exactly why I loved it so much."* —**Will Shortz**

To order, call: 1 (800) 343-4499 www.emmisbooks.com

TURN THAT DOWN!

A Hysterical History of Rock, Roll, Pop, Soul, Punk, Funk, Rap, Grunge, Motown, Metal, Disco, Techno, *and* Other Forms *of* Musical Aggression through the Ages • Lewis Grossberger

emmis humor

www.emmisbooks.com/humor

What are YOU laughing at?

(513) 861-4045

The Old Firehouse 1700 Madison Rd. Cincinnati, OH 45206

© 2005 Emmis Humor

emmis humor